Afghanistan

A CULTURAL HISTORY

Afghanistan

A CULTURAL HISTORY

St John Simpson

INTERLINK BOOKS
An imprint of Interlink Publishing Group, Inc.

First published in 2012 by

INTERLINK BOOKS
An imprint of Interlink Publishing Group, Inc.
46 Crosby Street, Northampton, Massachusetts 01060
www.interlinkbooks.com

Library of Congress Cataloging-in-Publication Data available

ISBN: 978-1-56656-854-8

Book design by Zoë Mellors

Frontispiece: The mausoleum of Ahmad Shah Durrani
at Kandahar (see p. 137 for full caption).
Page 4: Stone calf-head pommel. Achaemenid or Hellenistic,
4th–3rd century BC. L. 6 cm. British Museum, 1936,0613.234.

Printed and bound in Grafos S.A., in Spain

To request our complete 48-page full-color catalog, please call us toll
free at 1-800-238-LINK, visit our website at www.interlinkbooks.com,
or send us an e-mail: info@interlinkbooks.com

The papers used in this book are recyclable products made from wood grown in well-managed
forests and other controlled sources. The manufacturing processes conform to the
environmental regulations of the country of origin.

Contents

UZBEKISTAN

TURKMENISTAN

KOPET DAGH RANGE

Amu Darya (Oxus)

Tash Gozar • Termez

Bactra ■
Balkh •

■ Tillya
Tepe

Mazar-e
Sharif

Samang

(Murghab)

Murgap

Torkestan Mountains

Konduz

Buddhas of
Bamiyan ■
Bamiyan •

Hari Rud

• Herat (Hirat)

Bayan Range

Koh-e Baba Rang

• Panjab

HAZARAJAT

I R A N

A F G H A N I S T A

Naomid
Plain

Khash
Desert PUSHT-I-RUD

• Sangin

SĪSTĀN

S Ī S T A N B A S I N

• Lashkar Gah

• Kandahar

R e g i s t a n

Tob

Helmand

Map of Afghanistan
marking some of the
many places mentioned
in the text.

Chagai Hills

PAKISTAN

TAJIKISTAN

Pamirs

CHINA

Wakhan Mts.

Aï Khanum

Kunduz
(Kondoz)

H I N D U   K U S H

Karakorum Range

Tepe Fullol

urkh Kotal

Chitral

Panjshir

P A K I S T A N

Panjshir

Jabal os Saraj
Shotorak
Bagram

Nuristan

H I M A L A Y A

KABUL
(Kabol)

Jalalabad

Hadda

Khyber Pass

SRINAGAR

Vale of Kashmir

I N D I A

Pir Panjal Range

PESHAWAR

Indus

Islamabad

Gardiz

RAWALPINDI

Khost
(Khowst)

Gujrat

N

Kakar Range

Aï Khanum ■ Featured historic site

Bactra ■ Other historic site

0 _____ 200 km
0 _____ 100 miles

Introduction: Afghanistan, the Crossroads of Asia

Afghanistan, with its rich and ancient history – and its pivotal position at one of the proverbial crossroads of Asia – is an excellent illustration of how cultures and people are shaped by geography and the changing circumstances of politics, economy and religion. Developments within Afghanistan are closely interlocked with those in the major neighbouring regions of what are now Pakistan, India, China, Iran and the Central Asian states of Turkmenistan, Uzbekistan and Tajikistan, and to reconstruct its history at any period means looking at its changing relationship with its neighbours.

There are three main ways of approaching this. Archaeology provides a fundamental source of information on reconstructing cultural history and the flow of fashions, ideas and trade, and it remains the only source for many periods. Unfortunately, while there were some important early antiquarian researches in the nineteenth century, and there have always been chance finds, systematic archaeological surveys and excavations only began in 1922 and this work was interrupted until the early years of this century by the Soviet invasion in 1979 and the decades of conflict that followed. The study of individual rulers as portrayed on their coins has been a further traditional way of reconstructing local political history in the late pre-Islamic period, although it is rarely linked to the archaeological context. Finally, the writings of Classical historians, medieval Islamic scholars, Chinese authors and later travellers provide valuable descriptions of the peoples, places and objects they saw or heard about.

There are a growing number of studies on Afghanistan as attempts are made to better understand a country that is regularly in the news. Most either dwell on the conflict, politics or culture of the past two centuries or survey the archaeology and architecture of the pre-Islamic and Islamic periods within the modern political borders of Afghanistan. This book is neither of these, nor is it a story told by coins, a history book, a study of the art of the region or the legacy of Alexander – such books already exist. Instead this short account offers a glimpse into the world of Afghanistan and its evolving culture and history by taking and combining some of the most relevant pieces of evidence, whether historical or archaeological. It is necessarily sketchy and summarized, yet

The only known source of lapis lazuli in the ancient world was Afghanistan. The lapis beads here date to about 2500 BC and were found at Ur in southern Iraq. British Museum, 1928,1010.202.

View of the fertile Bamiyan Valley taken from the remains of the 11th century medieval city of Bamiyan, known today as *Shahr-i Gholghola* ('City of Murmurs'). Photo: Warwick Ball.

it attempts to show that to appreciate Afghanistan the country should be viewed not only over a long period but also within its wider regional context. Cultural and modern political borders are not the same and it would be a great mistake to assume they are. Over the course of the last few thousand years Afghanistan has enjoyed close relations with its neighbours. These have varied in strength and direction at different periods between India, Iran or Central Asia; they have been peaceful at times, warring at others. However, when conditions have allowed, Afghanistan has developed a thriving economy based on its rich resources and cross-cultural contacts. This is an important lesson, and a model of what the future might hold.

Shaping Afghanistan: geography and resources

The physical geography of Afghanistan, together with its valuable natural resources, has undoubtedly helped to shape its history. While the control and exploitation of its resources at different periods helps to explain some of the sources of wealth and power in Afghanistan, its geographical position where many routes cross at the heart of Asia explains another critical feature of its history. It is a mountainous region rich in valuable metal and mineral resources. Its interconnected valleys allow flocks to be moved between lowland and highland pastures depending on the seasons. It is landlocked, but closely connected by its natural geography to its modern neighbours of Iran to the west, Pakistan to the south and east and Turkmenistan, Uzbekistan, Tajikistan and China to the north. Routes criss-cross the country and have funnelled the movement of many peoples, whether Iranians, Greeks, Turks, Mongols, Russians or British. Control of Afghanistan has provided both a route to the fertile lands of the south-east and a means of protecting this valuable route. Afghanistan is easy to enter or to cross, but much more difficult to hold, let alone unite, because of this very geography.

The country today covers some 647,500 square kilometres, an area larger than France. Its borders were defined in the late-nineteenth century and were mostly based on political rather than geographical considerations, cutting through traditional tribal lands and taking little account of traditional allegiances. We shall see how and why this happened in Chapter eight (p. 140).

Rainfall varies hugely throughout Afghanistan and so the landscapes vary accordingly from stony or sandy desert in the south and west, to open woodland on the Hindu Kush mountain range, fertile loess (silt sediment) on the northern plains and semi-tropical vegetation in the east around Jalalabad. Most of the country is above 1,000 metres and semi-desertic – that is, between desert terrain and woodland – and it is effectively almost bisected by the high mountains of the Hindu Kush. The great medieval traveller and Islamic scholar ibn Battuta (1304–77), a Moroccan

Berber whose travels took him as far afield as Europe in the west and China and South East Asia in the east, stated that these mountains are 'called Hindu Kush, which means "Slayer of Indians", because the slave boys and girls who are brought from India die there in large numbers as a result of the extreme cold and the quantity of snow'. The name Hindu Kush is also explained as meaning, more prosaically, 'mountains of India.' The mountains cover most of the central and eastern parts of the country, are rich in mineral deposits and effectively divide the country into two. Controlling the routes through the Hindu Kush has always been critical for rulers wishing to unify the country and exploit these resources.

Lower mountains and foothills extend north and south of the Hindu Kush. The northern region is potentially fertile because of the thick deposits of loess blown south from the Central Asian steppe. The richest agricultural lands are around Herat and along the Hari Rud river in the west, Kunduz and Mazar-i Sharif in the north, Kabul and Jalalabad in the east, and around Kandahar on the upper Helmand river in the south-east. The northern plains contain small oases created by rivers flowing north from the Hindu Kush, which form fan-like deltas before reaching the Amu Darya (the ancient river Oxus) to the north. The largest oasis contains the city of Balkh, known as the 'Mother of Cities' and the 'dome of Islam', and which was also described in medieval sources as being surrounded by gardens producing oranges, lilies, grapes, raisins, almonds and other nuts, sugar cane, sesame and rice. Turmeric, unguents, clarified butter, syrups and a type of preserve made from pomegranate kernel were also exported from the city, whereas the city of Termez (now in Uzbekistan) on the opposite bank of the Amu Darya was known for its excellent grapes and quinces. Further east, the town of Samangan was described as a centre for the cultivation of corn, cotton and grapes, while the Kunduz district was known for its corn, grapes, figs, peaches and pistachios.

The main river in the south is the Helmand which is flanked by the stony northern Dasht-i Margo ('Desert of Death') and sandy southern deserts (Registan). The tenth-century Iranian geographer al-Istakhri praised the fertility of this region and the abundance of dates, grapes, other foodstuffs and asafoetida (which was used as a universal seasoning). His contemporary al-Tha°alibi singled out its plums and figs as 'of a quality unmatched elsewhere', adding his praise of the town of Bost (Afghanistan):

> In all the countries of the earth which I have travelled through, I have never seen one superior to Bost in beauty, healthiness, abundance of provisions, dates, sweet-smelling herbs and cultivated vegetables. I firmly believe that whoever dies at Bost, having the assurance of divine forgiveness, is simply transported from one garden of paradise to another.

Water supply is critical not only for settled communities reliant on agriculture, but also for those communities relying on herding or hunter-gathering. As late as the 1960s it was estimated that some ninety per cent of the Afghan population was rural, three-quarters of them living in settled villages (although there has since been a considerable drift into the towns as well as emigration as a result of the past decades of conflict). Most of these villages were concentrated in the plains and lowlands, either along rivers or in oases. Only some twelve per cent of the country can be cultivated, however, and most of this land requires irrigation. Permanent settlement, whether ancient or modern, is therefore concentrated in a relatively small portion of the country, and there is great pressure on both land and water. As a result, controlling these particular zones has been – and continues to be – of high political importance.

In the past the main staple crops were wheat and barley, but opium and cannabis now yield much higher economic returns. Animal husbandry is widely practised and based on mixed flocks of sheep and goats, since Islam prohibits the consumption of pork and the general scarcity of water prevents large herds of cattle being raised. Chickens are also common. Seasonal migration of livestock enables use of mountain pastures in the spring and summer, and their produce (whether meat, dairy, hair or wool) has traditionally been exchanged or sold by nomads and semi-nomads for grain, vegetables, fruit and other products offered by settled communities. The antiquity of this economic pattern is unclear, although in the early first century AD Greek historian and geographer Strabo, probably following an earlier lost account, commented that:

> *Aria* [the Herat province] *and Margiana* [the Merv oasis of neighbouring Turkmenistan] *are the most powerful districts in this part of Asia, these districts in part being enclosed by the mountains and in part having their habitations in the plains. Now the mountains are occupied by tent-dwellers, and the plains are intersected by rivers that irrigate them, partly by the Arius* [Hari Rud] *and partly by the Margus* [Murghab].

In medieval times, the western district of Balkh, around Guzgan (roughly centred on modern Gurziwan in northern Afghanistan's Faryab Province) – an area of steppe and fertile pasture – was well known for its export of tanned hides, whereas the town of Taliqan

in north-east Afghanistan was famous for its felts in the ninth century, and wool was a major source of revenue for the Rukhkhaj district near Kandahar. It is easy to underestimate both the antiquity and the economic importance of agricultural industries such as these, but they are a mainstay of the local economy today and probably have been for a very long time.

Metals, minerals and precious stones

Afghanistan is rich in metals and minerals including gold, silver, bronze, copper, spinel rubies and the extremely rare lapis lazuli. The sale of such precious commodities contributed to local wealth and doubtless also the status of those who controlled their exploitation. The tributaries of the Amu Darya contain gold-bearing sands, which were probably exploited from early antiquity. In his treatise *On the Nature of Animals*, the second-century Roman author Aelian recognized that there was a source of gold in Bactria (a historical region that is now part of Afghanistan, Uzbekistan and Tajikistan), although he also believed this to be the home of the

View of the Hindu Kush from the south, taken near the Salang Pass. Photo: Bill Woodburn

legendary griffin, a mythical beast with the head and wings of an eagle and the body of a lion. Medieval authors reported gold mines in the mountains near Bamiyan and north of Panjshir; gold is also found near Muqqur, north-east of Kandahar, and a medieval history of southern Afghanistan, known as the *Tarikh-i Sistan*, refers to the panning of gold in a tributary of the Helmand. The American explorer Colonel Alexander Gardner (1785–1877) visited the region in the nineteenth century and noted that the people of this area were generally herdsmen or farmers, but supplemented their income by panning in the rivers.

North-east Afghanistan is a major source of silver and this has been exploited for thousands of years. Early Islamic writers reported silver mines in the mountains near Bamiyan and Badakhshan, particularly in the Panjshir and the Wakhan valleys. The tenth-century writer ibn Hawqal described the miners as unruly folk, and the geographer Yaqut writing in the early thirteenth century describes how they worked by torchlight, but freely gambled their proceeds away. The Venetian merchant Marco Polo (c.1254–1324) also describes the mines as being very productive in the late thirteenth century, but they had already been abandoned when ibn Battuta visited in 1333.

Copper ores are common throughout the country, especially in the Logar valley south of Kabul, south-west of Herat, north of Kandahar, and north of the Panjshir. There is extensive archaeological evidence for the use of copper in Afghanistan, where it was used to make small objects such as seals, weapons and containers from at least the third millennium BC. The origins of these local industries are probably even earlier as the smelting of copper is attested from as early as the fifth millennium BC in neighbouring Iran.

Beginning in the third millennium BC, tin was sought after as an alloying material added to copper to make bronze. Clay tablets written in cuneiform script in ancient Mesopotamia (modern Iraq) refer to the importation of tin from the east, and as none has been located in Iran, the most likely source of this is Afghanistan, where there are two extensive regions of tin deposits – one extending from Sistan towards Herat and the other extending from Badakhshan to Kandahar. In both cases tin occurs as cassiterite and is frequently associated with deposits of copper, gold and lead. Moreover, Strabo refers specifically to Drangiana (Sistan) as a source of tin in the first century AD.

Lead, vitriol and arsenic mines are recorded near Balkh by medieval geographers. In the ninth century, mercury and lead are mentioned from Bamiyan and crucible steel was produced in Herat. Finally, there are extensive iron ore deposits near the Hajigak pass west of Kabul.

In addition to these metallic ores, a range of minerals occurs in the mountains. The most famous is lapis lazuli, a very rare semi-precious stone with only one major source to be exploited in antiquity, near Sar-i Sang in the Kokcha valley of the north-eastern

Badakhshan region. Lapis lazuli has long been prized for its striking blue colour, and has been used to make small objects, inlays and the vivid blue pigment known as ultramarine. There are several lapis lazuli mines in operation in Afghanistan today. Three grades of lapis were defined on the basis of intensity of colour: one like indigo and the others light blue and green. In antiquity, the deep blue variety was considered the most valuable, and it was exported across the Near East from the late fourth millennium BC onwards, to be used for seals and personal adornments. New scientific research on pigments used in ancient Greece has also shown that it was being used as a rare pigment in the fifth century BC, much earlier than previously suspected; it must have been exported via the intervening Achaemenid Empire.

View of a lake in the Band-e Amir National Park in central Afghanistan. Photo: tropix.co.uk/ Jonathan Lee.

Badakhshan was also a source of pure rock crystal and bezoar stones, both used for inlays. Garnets were a popular source of inlay in local jewellery and finger rings during the first centuries AD. This

fashion extended northwards into Central Asia and westwards across the Sasanian and Byzantine empires, and into Europe, where garnets were widely used in Anglo-Saxon metalwork (although the exact source of these is the subject of ongoing scientific research). Finally, turquoise is said to occur at Kuh-i Dasht, south of Herat – although the famous source in ancient and medieval times was near Maden, in the Nishapur area of neighbouring north-east Iran. In any case, nomad grave goods recovered from Tillya Tepe in northern Afghanistan reveal that turquoise was used extensively as a source of jewellery inlay during the first century.

Islamic personal seal carved from garnet and originally set as the bezel in a finger ring. It is inscribed in Arabic with the personal name 'Sahl b. Sakan'. 8th–10th century, 1.1 x 0.7 cm. British Museum, 1880.3641, collected in Afghanistan by Charles Masson.

Its wealth of natural resources and its pivotal position among so many other civilizations and cultures explain why Afghanistan has been home to numerous indigenous, migrating or invading peoples at different times in history. In order to explore the various peoples of Afghanistan and their contributions, this book is arranged chronologically, at first relying entirely on archaeological evidence, the only kind that is available, and then increasingly using historical sources, interwoven with the revealing evidence of everyday objects to create a more balanced, cultural historical outline.

Chapter 1
Prehistory

Bronze axe-head found in a grave at Khinaman in south-east Iran: it belongs to a type which was made and used across south-east Iran, Afghanistan and southern Central Asia and dates to about 2000 BC. H. 12.5 cm; w. 15 cm. British Museum, 1913,1229.10, donated by Gen. Sir Percy Molesworth Sykes KCIE.

Our knowledge of the earliest periods of settlement and civilization in Afghanistan relies entirely on archaeology and much still remains to be understood. There is evidence for early Stone Age and later prehistoric activity in parts of the country but these earliest periods in Afghanistan are under-researched and the dating and distribution of sites are largely uncertain. However, as in other regions, there was probably a long gradual period of familiarization and experimentation with different local resources, whether plants or minerals, with bartering and the exchange of some materials between different communities, and from these roots grew the successful agricultural, manufacturing and trading economies of the subsequent Bronze Age during the third and second millennia BC.

More is known about the Bronze Age and how the ancient cultures in modern Afghanistan were very closely connected by culture and trade with their neighbours across the modern political borders. As in the periods that follow, it is clear that in order to understand developments inside modern Afghanistan's borders it is essential to combine the local archaeological evidence with that from what are now neighbouring countries. In 1951 French archaeologists began work at the site of Mundigak, north-west of Kandahar in southern Afghanistan. Their results showed its development from a small agricultural village dating to the beginning of the fourth millennium BC to an important urban centre with monumental architecture in the third millennium BC. This was the first major Bronze Age site to be excavated between the contemporary cities of the Indus Valley civilization (the Harappan) to the east and south (in what is now Pakistan and western India) and city-sites in south-west Iran and southern Mesopotamia to the west, yet at first the finds remained in cultural isolation, and so little could be learnt from them.

This began to change in the 1960s and 1970s, when Soviet archaeologists initiated large-scale surveys and excavations across

Fragmentary footed gold bowl from Tepe Fullol dating to about 2000 BC. The decoration of repeating stepped design is a typical ancient Central Asian motif which was probably inspired by woven rugs. Drawing by Philippe Gouin.

the southern republics of the Soviet Union. They reported sites dating from the seventh millennium BC onwards along the northern foot of the Kopet Dagh (the mountain range forming the frontier between Turkmenistan and Iran), with an increase in the number and size of these beginning in the early third millennium BC. Moreover, the progressively eastward distribution of archaeological sites suggested a gradual move into neighbouring regions, including the Merv Oasis and Bactria (a historical region that is now part of Afghanistan, Uzbekistan and Tajikistan). During the same period, Danish archaeologists working along the full length of the Persian Gulf between Kuwait and Oman discovered sites and objects such as seals, weights and pottery which proved the existence of maritime trade linking the Indus and Iran with Arabia and Mesopotamia. Large areas of southern and eastern Iran also began to be surveyed during these decades, and different settlements excavated for the first time since the earlier pioneering surveys by the Hungarian-British archaeologist Sir Aurel Stein (1862–1943), whose recently restored tombstone can be seen in Kabul. The results of all these investigations finally began to fill in gaps on the map around Afghanistan and to create a better cultural context for discoveries within Afghanistan itself.

Despite the earlier work at Mundigak in the south, little was known about the equivalent period in northern Afghanistan until, in July 1966, villagers discovered a group of gold and silver vessels

Bronze axe-head with silver inlays, showing a wild boar surprising a tiger in the act of leaping on a deer. The edge of the axe is at the bottom. Iran, c.2500–2000 BC. L. 17.8 cm. British Museum, 1913,0314.1, donated by Henry Oppenheimer through The Art Fund.

Fragmentary copper alloy seal in the form of a big cat; this would have been used to mark personal property. Bactria, Afghanistan, c.2000 BC. H. 3.5 cm; w. 7.1 cm. British Museum, 1993,0619.1, donated by Simon Digby.

at Khosh Tapa, better known as Tepe Fullol, in Badakhshan province. These probably belonged to a wealthy grave and were the first sign of significant Bronze Age life in northern Afghanistan. The reported findspot was investigated by an Afghan archaeologist, but in the absence of any other known sites of this period north of the Hindu Kush, parallels for the designs on the metalwares were at first sought with cultures in Central Asia, Iran and Mesopotamia and suggested dates ranged from 2600 to 1350 BC. Two years later Soviet archaeologists began to explore sites on the northern plains of Afghanistan and to compare the results with equivalent patterns of settlement in the southern republics of the Soviet Union. More than sixty-four Bronze Age sites, ranging from small villages and cemeteries to larger population centres, were mapped in north-west Afghanistan, providing the earliest evidence for ancient settlement patterns in this region. These sites fall into four clusters, which appear to represent ancient oases formed on the lower delta fans of the rivers Shirin Tagab and Balkhab. Not all were occupied at the same time, and some may have been occupied only briefly. Several pottery kilns and a lapis lazuli and turquoise workshop were also found, proving that these sites were directly engaged in the working of these semi-precious materials which were traded overland deeper into Central Asia and the Middle East. Extensive areas with surface scatters of pottery were also noted. These were initially thought to be regularly occupied campsites, but they may represent evidence for ancient manuring of fields, using the fertile earth dug from refuse heaps.

An extensive concentration of Bronze Age settlements was found in the Dashly oasis, which covers an area of about 100 square kilometres, and was originally watered by the river Balkhab. A small number of these were sufficiently large to be called towns and contained a fortified central complex, probably occupied by local elites, surrounded by an unwalled settlement. Stores of clay slingshot and carefully worked leaf-shaped flint arrowheads proved that the occupants had medium-range weapons, for hunting, warfare or both. The continuing use of chipped stone for these arrowheads, as well as blades and larger points, parallels the situation in Iraq and Syria where flint continued to be used for making arrowheads and utility tools long after the introduction of metal, and probably reflects the work of skilled professional craftsmen. Metal was also used for items of personal adornment, polished mirrors, cosmetic sets, cloak pins with decorative heads, compartmented seals, daggers, axe-heads, mace-heads, arrowheads, spatulae and choppers. These were either hammered or cast in clay moulds. Analyses of some bronze objects indicate that the quality of the metal – which contained either arsenic or lead, but not tin – was relatively soft and unsuited for weapons or cutting-edge tools, and some of the objects may therefore have been status symbols. Other finds included handmade coarse pottery, a small number of greyware spouted bowls and hemispherical cups,

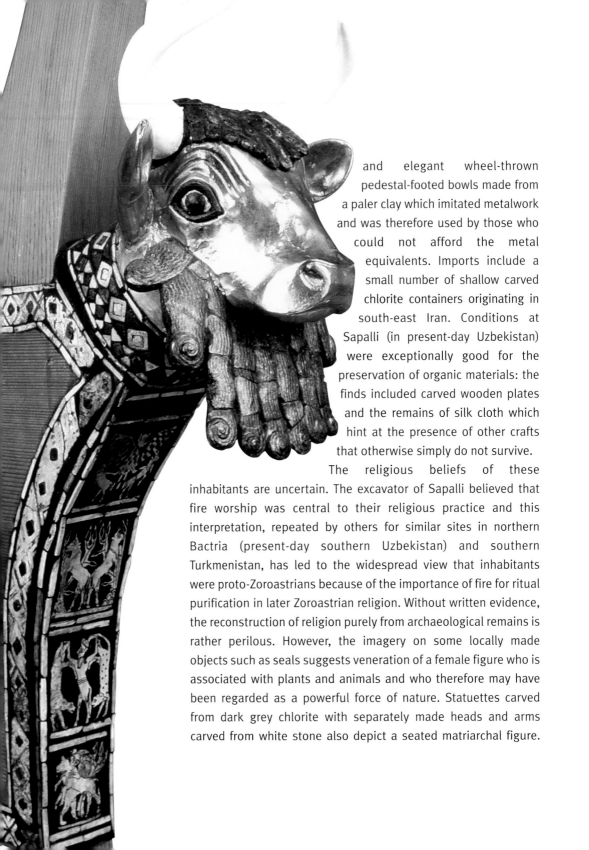

and elegant wheel-thrown pedestal-footed bowls made from a paler clay which imitated metalwork and was therefore used by those who could not afford the metal equivalents. Imports include a small number of shallow carved chlorite containers originating in south-east Iran. Conditions at Sapalli (in present-day Uzbekistan) were exceptionally good for the preservation of organic materials: the finds included carved wooden plates and the remains of silk cloth which hint at the presence of other crafts that otherwise simply do not survive.

The religious beliefs of these inhabitants are uncertain. The excavator of Sapalli believed that fire worship was central to their religious practice and this interpretation, repeated by others for similar sites in northern Bactria (present-day southern Uzbekistan) and southern Turkmenistan, has led to the widespread view that inhabitants were proto-Zoroastrians because of the importance of fire for ritual purification in later Zoroastrian religion. Without written evidence, the reconstruction of religion purely from archaeological remains is rather perilous. However, the imagery on some locally made objects such as seals suggests veneration of a female figure who is associated with plants and animals and who therefore may have been regarded as a powerful force of nature. Statuettes carved from dark grey chlorite with separately made heads and arms carved from white stone also depict a seated matriarchal figure.

Moreover, there does seem to be evidence for belief in an afterlife. The cemetery at the settlement now known as Dashly 1, in northern Afghanistan, consisted of pits containing burials accompanied by pottery vessels, and sealed with mud bricks, but richer graves were found near a large circular building. Copper pins, mirrors, bracelets, rings and carved stone vessels were among the objects found in these graves, implying that the inhabitants felt the need to place familiar household possessions for the deceased to use in an afterlife. Burial pits containing large numbers of pots but no bodies may have a memorial function, and resemble those commonly found in northern Bactria and the Merv Oasis. Moreover, at Dashly 1, two ritual burials of complete rams were found, each accompanied by several pots. Whether these represent substitute burials for people or some other custom is unclear. It has been suggested that there is little evidence for social hierarchy in these graves, but this partly reflects the Marxist approach of some Soviet researchers and the interpretation may be questioned in the light of the architectural evidence for fortified buildings and more recent discoveries in neighbouring Turkmenistan, discussed overleaf.

In 1974 French archaeologists working in northern Afghanistan's Amu Darya valley began to find Bronze Age sites on the Shortughai plain. The discovery of Harappan materials at Shortughai itself suggests that the Indus Valley civilization may have attempted to control the lucrative trade in semi-precious lapis lazuli sourced

Opposite Lapis lazuli beard inlay on a reconstructed Mesopotamian lyre excavated at Ur, southern Iraq, *c.*2600 BC. The source of the lapis is in Badakhshan, north-east Afghanistan. H. 112.5 cm; w. 73 cm. British Museum, 1928,1010.1.a.

Below Cylinder seal carved from high-quality lapis lazuli and engraved with a geometric design typical of south-east Iran. The seal dates to about 2500 BC and impressions of identical seals have been found at Ur in southern Iraq. L. 4.4 cm; diam. 0.8 cm. British Museum, 1936,0613.238.

Lapis lazuli was highly valued across the Middle East for thousands of years. This model hair comb was excavated in the Neo-Assyrian royal city of Tarbisu (modern Sherif Khan) in northern Iraq and dates to about the 9th century BC. L. 2 cm; w. 1.75 cm. British Museum, 1855,1205.470.

from the nearby mines at Sar-i Sang. The highest-quality lapis is deep blue and unmatched in appearance by any other natural material: it is not difficult to see how it might have acquired a magical status particularly as there was only one source of this stone throughout antiquity and this is, and probably always was, difficult to access.

Across the modern border in present-day Turkmenistan, new archaeological fieldwork has added to our understanding of the chronology and importance of these earlier finds from northern Afghanistan. It is now clear that the two regions shared the same material culture, and common elements in the burial customs suggest that they may have also had similar beliefs. This single cultural entity has been termed the 'Bactria-Margiana Archaeological Complex' and some scholars have recently sought to identify it with the region referred to in ancient Mesopotamian texts as Marhashi. The largest and most important site of this culture is called Gonur-depe, in the northern part of the Merv Oasis (present-day Turkmenistan). It is dominated by two large fortified complexes separated in ancient times by a watercourse, with a very extensive nearby cemetery of several thousand graves. Most of these graves contain a single burial accompanied by a few pots, but there are some exceptional burials that include silver vessels, beak-spouted copper alloy vessels, lapis lazuli beads, imported Iranian chlorite containers and Indus etched carnelian beads.

In 2003–4, a so-called 'royal cemetery' was discovered at Gonur-depe. Named after Sir Leonard Woolley's much earlier famous discoveries at Ur in southern Iraq, although without inscriptions to confirm the identity or rank of the deceased, the finds are nevertheless spectacular and open an exceptionally important window into the wealth and cultural complexity of the Bronze Age inhabitants of this region. They include four-wheeled carts with reinforced metal treads (identical to examples known from Iran) and accompanied by camels. There were gold and silver vessels, some with hammered decoration or engraved with some of the earliest depictions of two-humped camels, and one depicting a range of wild animals in a composition inspired by Mesopotamian art of the Akkadian dynasty (c.2350–2150 BC). Metal pins with elaborate floral or figural heads were found, along with inlaid panels, some apparently belonging to boxes or gaming boards, and others possibly even attached to the grave walls. The excavation uncovered large calcite discs of unknown function, but familiar from earlier finds at Tepe Hissar (Iran), Altyn-depe (Turkmenistan) and other sites in Central Asia, along with long stone ceremonial staffs or sceptres. There were locally produced copper-alloy seals and axes, quivers of flint-tipped arrows, small imported calcite vessels imitating the shape of metalwares, ivory dice of Indus type and chlorite lidded boxes imported from south-east Iran. The richness of the finds not only underlines the technical skill of local craftsmen but also illustrates the concentration of wealth and appropriation of foreign ideas by these local rulers.

A small number of other long-distance imports were found in the same cemetery. They include a heavily worn Mesopotamian stone weight in the form of a sleeping duck, a Mesopotamian cylinder seal of the Ur III dynasty (c.2100–2000 BC), and an Indus seal showing an elephant. A locally carved cylinder seal inspired by Mesopotamian art was found at a nearby site. Three more ivory long dice of Indus type were found in a room at Gonur-depe and thought to be used in fortune-telling, and others have been found at the large settlement site of Altyn-depe, close to the Kopet Dagh mountains that separate Turkmenistan from Iran. The discovery of items associated with the Bactria-Margiana Archaeological Complex along Afghanistan's upper Murghab valley, Gulran near Herat and on the opposite side of the Kopet Dagh – in Iran near Bujnurd and in the Gurgan plain – suggests that cultural and trade connections extended across the modern political borders. By contrast, the discovery of small sites with different styles of handmade pottery, hint at the beginning of long-term relationships between local settled and nomadic or semi-nomadic populations originating further north.

No evidence for writing has been found at Gonur-depe although symbols incised on pottery vessels have been interpreted as pictograms. The identity of the ruling class is therefore unknown, as is the function of the fortified buildings. They have been interpreted as a sacred royal complex devoted to the worship of fire and water, and connected with a population who practised a form of Zoroastrianism. Central to this hypothesis was the identification of carbonized seed impressions as the remains of the plants ephedra and hemp which, according to some authors, were used in the preparation of the hallucinogenic drink *soma-haoma* described in Zoroastrian religious texts. However, both the botanical and the philological identifications have been challenged and the carbonized plant remains re-identified as millet. There is evidence for cultivated barley, wheat, pulses and grapes, offering a glimpse into the agricultual economy which was doubtless also practised by contemporary societies across northern Afghanistan where we lack the equivalent archaeological evidence at the moment.

It is now clear from this archaeological evidence that between the late third and early second millennia BC, the fertile regions of the Helmand valley, Bactria and Central Asian oases enjoyed massive economic growth, with trade connections to cities in the Indus Valley, eastern Iran and Mesopotamia. Afghanistan was a very rich source of raw materials including tin, copper, gold and lapis lazuli, all of which were in heavy demand during these periods, and it could have easily supplied the needs of its neighbouring regions. This economic boom within Afghanistan probably followed a long period of settled village life, with gradual domestication of plant and animal species contemporary with developments in eastern Iran and southern Turkmenistan where we have more information than from within Afghanistan itself. What happened next, during the late second and early first millennia BC, or Late Bronze and Early Iron Age, is unclear but it seems unlikely that the entire region was abandoned, especially as the overall settlement pattern remains very similar; further fieldwork and research may answer these questions. What is clear, however, is that when this region was incorporated into the Achaemenid Empire of Iran in the mid-first millennium BC it was to play an important role.

Chapter 2
Afghanistan under the Achaemenids

Achaemenid gold chariot model
from the Oxus Treasure, found
in the 19th century in Takht-i
Kuwad, immediately north of the
modern border of Afghanistan.
5th–4th century BC. H. 7 cm;
L. 19.5 cm. British Museum,
1897,1231.7, bequeathed by Sir
Augustus Wollaston Franks.

In 550 BC a powerful new individual entered history, creating the new world empire of the Achaemenids (*c*.550–330 BC) which ultimately stretched from present-day Libya to Pakistan, encompassing what is now Afghanistan. The individual in question was Cyrus II (r. 550–530 BC), also known as Cyrus the Great, a Persian from southern Iran whose genealogy is presented on the Babylonian clay cuneiform document known as the Cyrus Cylinder as: 'Son of Cambyses, Great King, King of Anshan, great-grandson of Teispes, Great King, King of Anshan, from a family [that has] always [exercised] kingship'.

Within two decades, Cyrus had conquered Iran, Anatolia (modern Turkey) and Mesopotamia (modern Iraq). He added the strategically positioned Bactria (now part of Afghanistan, Uzbekistan and Tajikistan), to his empire, defeated the Massagetae (a nomadic Scythian tribe) on the Syr darya (ancient Jaxartes) frontier in what is now Uzbekistan in about 546–540 BC, and appears to have established garrisons along the northern edge of the intervening Merv Oasis. Peace was temporary, however; the ancient Greek historian Herodotus (*c*.484–425 BC) commented: 'When power changed hands, the states that until then were tributary to the Medes [ancient Iranian people] believed their situation also to be changed and revolted against Cyrus, and this defection was for Cyrus the cause and origin of numerous wars.' In 530 BC Cyrus was killed somewhere near the Aral Sea, probably fighting the Massagetae. Some years later, Darius I (r. 521–486 BC) came to the Persian throne with the backing of the satraps or governors of Bactria and Arachosia (Kandahar in modern Afghanistan).

Darius commemorated his accession, and the putting down of numerous rebellions, on a monumental rock-cut relief at Bisitun above the main road connecting Mesopotamia with western Iran. The relief shows Darius facing a line of bound rebels, with inscriptions in three cuneiform languages – Old Persian, Neo-

Elamite and Akkadian – setting out his deeds and victories. The twenty-three nations and regions within his empire, including several within the area of modern Afghanistan, are also listed. These were governed by satraps on behalf of the Great King whose seats of power were at Persepolis, Susa, Ecbatana (all in Iran) and Babylon (Iraq). Bactria was one of the most important provinces, with its rich agricultural and other resources, including gold and lapis lazuli, and control of trade routes across northern Afghanistan. Once the Achaemenids took control of Bactria, the province was governed from the city of Bactra (presumed to be Balkh) by members of the royal family, and appears to have had a powerful autonomous role throughout the reigns of Darius and Xerxes I (r. 485–465 BC). The Bisitun relief inscription illustrates the close connection between the administration of northern Afghanistan and southern Central Asia, and the Merv Oasis enters history under its older name of Margiana:

> . . . *a country, Margiana by name, that became rebellious to me.* [There was] *one single man, Frada by name, a Margian – him they made* [their] *chief. After that I sent – a Persian, Dadarshi by name, my vassal, satrap in Bactria – to him . . . Afterwards Dadarshi with the army marched off,* [and] *he fought a battle with the Margians . . . After that the country became mine. This* [is] *what has been done by me in Bactria.*

Evidence for Darius' claims of suppression has been sought in the archaeological record but remains inconclusive. What has been confirmed by archaeological surveys on either side of the Amu Darya (Oxus river), however, is a well-developed pattern of settlement and irrigation systems across Bactria. Some of these sites were large, and many were fortified although none are very precisely dated and some may be pre-Achaemenid foundations. They include the enormous citadels known as the Bala Hissar of Bactra (later known as Balkh), Altin Dilyar, the Bala Hissar in Kunduz, the nearby polygonal site of Qunsai and the central citadel of Dilberjin. At the site of Altin-10, a rectangular 'palace' was found consisting of two buildings: one with a fourteen-column portico on either side, the other with long narrow storerooms surrounding a central courtyard.

One of the greatest archaeological discoveries in northern Bactria is the Oxus Treasure, a spectacular collection of around 180 items and a large number of additional coins discovered between 1876 and 1880 on the northern bank of the river Amu Darya at a site called Takht-i Kuwad, situated close to the confluence of the Vakhsh and Pyandzh rivers. The Treasure offers the strongest evidence yet seen for the circulation of pieces made in a distinctive Persian style known as Achaemenid court style in a distant province such as Bactria. The location of Takht-i Kuwad at a confluence of rivers is similar to that of the later site of Ai Khanum (see p. 50), and seems to have been chosen for being naturally defensible.

The Oxus Treasure consists almost entirely of items of precious metal, gold, silver or gilded silver. It includes a large number of thin gold sheet plaques with engravings showing male (and very occasionally, female) dedicants grasping offerings, flowers or bundles of twigs resembling the traditional barsoms used by Zoroastrian priests in sacred ceremonies. One Russian scholar has interpreted a small number of fragmentary gold-covered iron rods from the same collection as symbolic barsoms, in other words further evidence that some of these objects were intended to be dedicated to a temple. The Treasure is also rich in personal adornments, including bracelets, armlets, neck rings, beads and clothing appliqués; many of these are incomplete, missing their

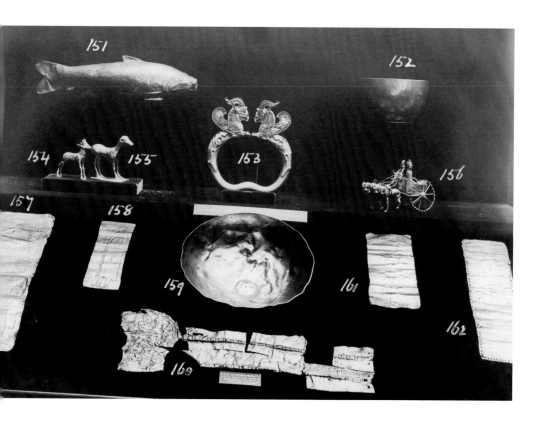

original coloured inlays of semi-precious stones and glass, or cut and twisted. When the pieces were first published in 1905, it was suggested that this damage was the result of later robbers attempting to divide their spoils, but the possibility remains that some may reflect ancient recycling before the treasure was hidden in one or more hoards of 'hacksilber' (literally, 'chopped silver' which was hoarded for its value by weight). Scientific analyses of some of the gold objects from the Oxus Treasure show that they were made using native alluvial gold. Although the origin of gold cannot be sourced, it is strongly possible that some of these

Part of the Oxus Treasure as it was first displayed at the British Museum c.1900. The display includes the gold scabbard (also shown on p. 40) before it was restored. Photo: British Museum.

objects were made in Bactria, and the exploitation of gold-bearing sands from the upper Amu Darya (as well as lapis lazuli from Badakhshan) is hinted at in Darius' Foundation Charter (a tablet inscribed in Old Persian) from his palace at Susa (in south-west Iran):

And gold from Sardis and Bactria was brought, that which was worked here. And the precious stones which [were] lapis lazuli and also carnelian, which were worked here, from Sogdiana were brought.

A few items in the Oxus Treasure are in different styles, including a pair of bracelets and a brooch that are similar to the 'Animal Style' art of the Scythians, the ancient Iranian nomadic peoples who ranged the steppes from what are now Mongolia and southern Siberia to as far west as the Black Sea. Others are likely to have been imported from other parts of the Persian Empire. Among these is a gilt-silver figure of a nude standing youth wearing a tall cap, which may have been part of a larger composition because the back of the figure was designed to be set up against a right-angled surface. He appears to have originally been holding reins; his headdress and the style of his torso resemble chariot axle pins from contemporary burial mounds near Sardis in western Turkey, and the object may therefore have been manufactured in this westernmost province of the Achaemenid Empire. The Oxus Treasure therefore appears to encompass types of object used in the Persian court, pieces dedicated to a local religious cult, and others imported from western provinces as well as possibly beyond the empire to the north. Although the objects were not found in archaeological contexts, the quantity of precious gold and silver objects suggests a high degree of disposable wealth.

The remainder of Afghanistan was divided into the provinces of

Aria (centred on Herat), Sattagydia (the central mountain region), Gandhara (Peshawar and possibly the Kabul region), Arachosia (Kandahar) and Zranka or Drangiana (Sistan), but little is yet known archaeologically about the Achaemenid period in many of these. However, the ancient site of Old Kandahar, a few kilometres south-west of modern Kandahar, was explored by a British expedition between 1974 and 1978. The excavations suggest that it was founded as a fortified city during the early or mid-first millennium BC, possibly replacing the earlier centre at Mundigak (see p. 22), and the fortifications were rebuilt probably during the Achaemenid period. This therefore may have been the capital of Arachosia, then known by the Iranian name of Harauvatish and whose representatives shown on Achaemenid royal monuments at Naqsh-i Rustam and Persepolis wore Iranian-style costumes. Two clay tablets inscribed in Elamite were excavated at the site and support the idea that this was an administrative centre. Moreover, Elamite tablets excavated at Persepolis and dated between 509 and 494 BC include references to officials who authorized payments to travellers from (or via) Arachosia and Bactria, and Aramaic inscriptions on ritual pestles, mortars and plates found in the Persepolis Treasury refer to three different places associated with treasurers from Arachosia. According to Darius I's foundation inscription from Susa, Arachosia was a source of ivory for the Achaemenid court, reflecting its proximity to India, and a variety of ivory objects including hair combs and inlays were even found in an Achaemenid palace well at Susa. Although nothing of this quality was found in the excavations at Old Kandahar, the pottery included a very distinctive shape of drinking bowl that is found across the entire Achaemenid Empire from Turkey to Pakistan. The popularity of these suggests that the high ritual and social importance to the Achaemenids of feasting and banqueting were recognized across the empire, and cheap pottery was substituted for metal in the case of poorer households emulating the elites.

Finally, archaeological surveys along the lower Helmand and excavations at the important site of Dahan-i Ghulaman, close to an ancient course of the Helmand river delta and across the modern border in Iran, throw some light on this period in the province of Zranka. Dahan-i Ghulaman must have been the administrative centre of the province and was almost a mile in length. Seven large buildings have been partly excavated and an area of private housing located. Other buildings share similarities with Achaemenid architecture at Persepolis (the ceremonial capital of the Achaemenid Empire) and Pasargadae (founded by Cyrus the Great) in the symmetrical use of columned porticoes, although they differ in not having any internal columns. Instead the architecture relies on mudbrick and heavily rammed clay (pakhsa), with vaulting using a technique of mudbrick struts. This technique is also seen at the earlier Median Iron Age settlement of Tepe Nush-i Jan in western Iran and continued in later Parthian architecture, notably at Shahr-i Qumis (once the capital of Parthia) in north-east Iran: it therefore appears to be of Iranian origin. Recent Iranian excavations have also revealed rare evidence for Achaemenid wall paintings, including the polychrome scene of a boar hunt by chariot. The pottery from Dahan-i Ghulaman includes cylindrical-conical beakers also known from excavations and surface collections at the nearby site of Nad-i Ali in lower Helmand, as well as from other sites in southern Turkmenistan and Bactria: these distinctive vessels may have been used for drinking. Other finds include small copper alloy arrowheads: these were the most common type at this period and were inspired by types used by Central Asian archers with powerful composite bows.

Overall, the evidence from this period in Afghanistan suggests that much of the material culture such as architecture, pottery and everyday items was little affected by the Achaemenid Empire, but that members of the elite closely followed the 'court style'. The style of the ruling class was, however, aped in the production of cheap pottery versions of metal drinking bowls. But a powerful empire encompassing the entire region from Egypt to what is now Pakistan must have brought more significant local benefits: people and ideas could travel more easily, and there was a common language of Aramaic, both spoken and written. Some scholars have argued that, as a result, Mesopotamian knowledge of astronomy spread to India during this period. The existence of fortified centres across Afghanistan and a dense rural population supported by well-irrigated agriculture implies an effective administration sustained by a complex balance of taxation and gift-giving which simultaneously cemented political ties and acknowledged local elites. The extent to which this was an Achaemenid innovation or an extension of earlier practice is unclear.

In 330 BC the retreating Darius III (r. 336–330 BC) was murdered on the Tehran plain by his eastern commanders, a deed attributed to Barsaentes, governor of Arachosia (Kandahar) and Satibarzanes, governor of Aria (Herat). In the meantime, Bessus, Darius' former general and

Opposite The restored gold scabbard (or sword sheath) from the Oxus Treasure. Achaemenid, 5th century BC. L. 27.6 cm. British Museum, 1897,1231.22, bequeathed by Sir Augustus Wollaston Franks.

Left and below Achaemenid lapis lazuli stamp seal excavated at Dilbat in southern Iraq, with its modern impression. It is engraved with a pair of human-headed winged monsters with scorpion bodies and lions' paws. 6th–4th century BC. Diam. 2.3 cm. British Museum, 1881,1103.1902.

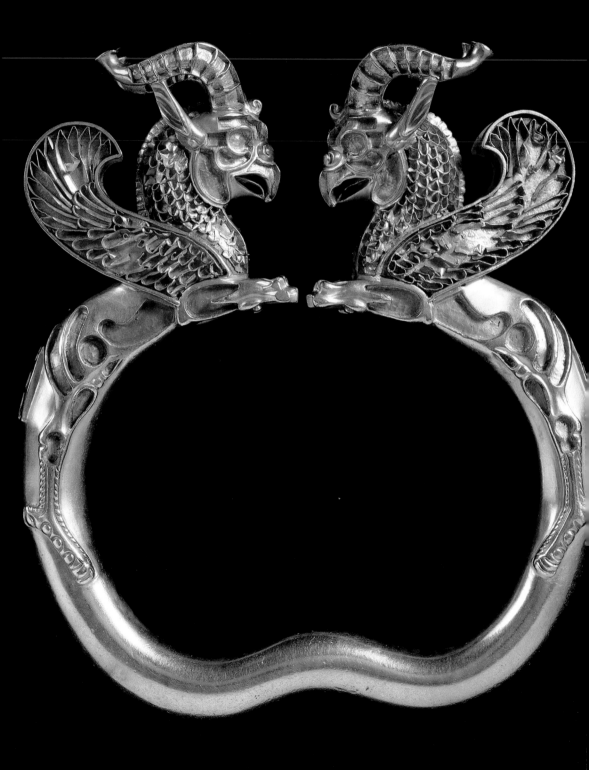

governor of Bactria, emerged as the leader and declared himself Artaxerxes IV, the legitimate successor to Darius. This was a real threat to Alexander the Great (356–323 BC), and the first century AD Roman writer Quintus Curtius Rufus claimed that Bactria could mobilize 30,000 horsemen. Aria initially feigned submission but the occupying Macedonian garrison was slaughtered and the region flared in revolt. An Iranian satrap was appointed as a replacement but he too sided with the rebels and Alexander was obliged to replace him with a Macedonian before marching through southern Afghanistan to subdue Arachosia. He then crossed the Hindu Kush into Bactria where Bessus was eventually captured in the summer of 329 BC. Further revolts drew Alexander into more bloody warfare north of the Oxus before he turned his sights eastwards towards India.

Alexander took Rauxnaka ('Little Star', pronounced *Roxane* by the Greeks), the daughter of the northern Bactrian warlord Oxyartes, as his bride, and adopted local dress. He continued his previous policy of initially appointing Iranians as satraps – including Proexes in the Hindu Kush region and Artabazos in Bactria – but Greco-Macedonian officers and troops now reinforced these officials, and the Macedonian Amyntas soon replaced Artabazos. In the case of Arachosia, a Macedonian named Menon was made satrap after his Iranian predecessor Barzaentes fled to India. This process continued with the appointment of Macedonians as satraps of the combined regions of Aria and Sistan, Gedrosia and Arachosia, and Parapomisos (as the Greeks now called the Hindu Kush). The implanting of a stronger Macedonian presence in the region helps to explain the strength of the local Hellenistic tradition that followed under the Seleucid Empire (312–363 BC) and Greco-Bactrian kingdom (*c.*250–125 BC).

Achaemenid gold armlet from the Oxus Treasure: the recessed areas on the two winged griffins originally contained coloured inlays. 5th–4th century BC. H. 12.3 cm; w. 11.6 cm. British Museum, 1897,1231.116, bequeathed by Sir Augustus Wollaston Franks.

Chapter 3

Greeks in the East:
Alexander and his Successors

Gandharan soapstone dish with a scene of the Greek goddess Aphrodite chastising Eros, the god of love. *c.* 1st or 2nd century and found in north-west Pakistan, possibly the Peshawar district. Diam. 12.3 cm. British Museum, 1973,0618.1.

Alexander the Great died in Babylon aged thirty-two on the night of 11 June 323 BC according to a Babylonian astronomical observation. His overthrow of the Achaemenid dynasty placed him as its successor in control of an empire that stretched from Greece to the Punjab and which included Afghanistan. When Alexander died, there was no credible local successor, as most of the senior administrators and generals were Greco-Macedonian, nor had he designated an heir. The immediate aftermath was civil war until his legacy was effectively divided between his generals.

Seleucus I (r. 312–281 BC), who had been an officer in Alexander's army and was once governor of Babylon, took control of most of the Middle East and thus founded what is known as the Seleucid Empire. He established his authority in Bactria in 305 BC but Chandragupta (c.321–297 BC), the ruler of the Mauryan kingdom in northern India, had already seized the Punjab and most of Afghanistan south of the Hindu Kush. Seleucus was obliged to acknowledge this through a peace treaty with Chandragupta where he gained 500 war elephants in exchange, and southern Afghanistan remained under Mauryan control for over a century.

At some point after about 250 BC, Diodotus I (c.250–230 BC), governor of Bactria under Antiochus II (286–246 BC), revolted and established his own independent Greek kingdom encompassing Bactria and Margiana, with his capital at Bactra (modern Balkh). The beginning of the Greco-Bactrian kingdom marked a clear political break from the Seleucid Empire although both shared Hellenistic culture. Diodotus' son Diodotus II succeeded him, followed in turn by Euthydemus I (235–200 BC). The latter was defeated in battle near Herat by the Seleucid ruler Antiochus III, who initially did not recognize the legitimacy of Euthydemus' rule. He was besieged in his capital for two years until the two rulers agreed a truce based on Euthydemus offering protection for both against the nomads. Euthydemus therefore continued in Bactria as ruler of the Greco-Bactrian kingdom, while Antiochus extended a peace treaty *c.*206 BC with the neighbouring Mauryan ruler Sophagasenus.

In the mid-second century BC, the Greco-Bactrian king Eucratides I (*c.*170–145 BC) campaigned south of the Hindu Kush against his Indo-Greek rival Menander and brought back considerable booty, the remains of which were found in the excavated treasury of the palace at Ai Khanum (and are discussed further on p. 53). He also campaigned northwards and extended his border from the so-called 'Iron Gates' near Derbend to Samarkand (Maracanda), in what is now Uzbekistan, where the city defences show archaeological evidence of rebuilding. The later Roman historian and author Justin (third century AD) summarized these events, based on an earlier account by Pompeius Trogus, as follows:

> *Eucratides engaged in several wars with great spirit, and though much reduced by his losses in them, yet, when he was besieged by Demetrius* [II] *king of the Indians, he repulsed a force of 60,000 enemies, by continual sallies with a garrison of only 300 soldiers. Having accordingly escaped after a siege of five months, he subjugated India. But as he was returning thence, he was assassinated on his march by his son* [Eucratides II] *with whom he had shared his throne.*

This took place *c.*145 BC, and the kingdom rapidly entered crisis. The Greek historian and geographer Strabo (*c.*64 BC–*c.* AD 24), writing during the time of the Roman Empire, refers to how 'a part of Bactriana was taken away from Eucratides by the Parthians'. The city of Merv was probably lost to Phraates II (*c.*138–127 BC), the first Parthian ruler to strike coins there. For the next few centuries, Merv was to control the north-eastern approaches to Iran from Central

Asia. Merv was part of the powerful Parthian state whose first ruler Mithradates I (*c*.171–138 BC) conquered most of the Seleucid Empire and whose capital was finally established at Ctesiphon, in what is now Iraq, opposite the previous eastern Seleucid capital of Seleucia-on-the-Tigris.

In the meantime, two waves of Central Asian nomads overran eastern Bactria, sacking the Greco-Bactrian frontier city of Ai Khanum on both occasions. According to the excavators, the first wave took place *c*.145 or 144 BC and its members were of Scythian origin, while the second wave of nomads probably corresponds to the Da Yuezhi of the Chinese sources or the Tokhari of later classical writers, and arrived in about 130 BC. The Chinese traveller and imperial envoy under the Han Dynasty, Zhang Qian, described the situation shortly afterwards, in 128–126 BC, as follows:

> *The inhabitants have fixed abodes and live in fortified towns and houses of regular form as in Fergana. They have neither a great chief or king, but all the cities have their own local dynasty. Although the people are skilled traders, their soldiers are weak and afraid of combat, so much so that when the Da Yuezhi ventured forth towards the west, they defeated the Da Xia* [Bactrians or Tokharians], *who became their subjects.*

Meanwhile, the region south of the Hindu Kush continued to be ruled by Greek kings. These rulers are conventionally called 'Indo-Greek' by modern scholars as they began striking coins with bilingual legends in Greek and Prakrit (the language of north-west India), which was initially written in Brahmi and then in Kharoshthi script. Some of these coins circulated in Bactria, and a large hoard has been found at Kunduz, but this does not prove that these rulers continued to control enclaves here as some have suggested.

Classical writers refer to Alexander creating a rich urban legacy in the east, with numerous cities bearing his name. The search for these cities inspired explorers as early as the nineteenth century but although some sites have yielded Greek pottery and coins, none of these identifications have been confirmed by inscriptions. The extent to which Alexander was able to found cities in the short space of time he had at his disposal is also rather controversial. Both Strabo (quoting the earlier Greek scholar Apollodorus) and Justin refer to Bactria as the land of a thousand cities, although Strabo had some doubts, but in any case several writers praised its fertility. Strabo commented that 'all writers, both ancient and modern, have praised the gentle climate and the fertility . . . of Bactria' and that 'Bactria produces everything, except olive oil'. Pliny the Elder (c. AD 23/4–79) wrote that 'the grains of corn are so large that a single one is like an ear of ours', and both Pliny and the Roman author Aelian (c. AD 170–235) describe how the 'camel of Bactria has two humps . . . and no incisors in its upper jaw', that it was used as a beast of burden, as well as in war, and that these beasts could 'move as fast as a horse, but their endurance is in proportion to their strength'. The Bactrian camel must have seemed wondrous indeed to those more used to seeing horses or donkeys in these roles.

The discovery of the city of Ai Khanum (a local Uzbek name meaning 'Moon Lady') in eastern Bactria revolutionized our understanding of how far Greek culture influenced the local population in northern Afghanistan. First identified as a site of unknown date in 1838, with Hellenistic remains reported by King Zahir Shah after a hunting trip in 1961, the site was extensively excavated by a French expedition directed by Paul Bernard between 1965 and 1978.

View of excavations in progress at Ai Khanum, with the collapsed remains of stone columns and their capitals. Photo: Delegation Archéologique Francaise en Afghanistan/ P. Bernard.

The site of the city was carefully selected for its natural defences. It lies at the confluence of the Kokcha and upper Amu Darya (Oxus river), and the riverbanks are some 20 metres high, providing the equivalent of the deep ditches favoured by Greek military planners. Fortifications surround all sides and included an outer ditch on the open north side, beyond which lay a burial ground. The triangular city is divided into three parts: a citadel, an upper city and a lower city with a long avenue down the centre. The date of foundation is uncertain, but was probably during the reign of Seleucus I, although there may be an earlier Achaemenid foundation on the citadel. The lower city was extensively excavated: it included a central administrative quarter and a residential quarter at the southern end. The northern area was not investigated, but may have been either an open area for livestock or seasonal nomads (evidence of both have been noted at Central Asian cities), or residential (perhaps explaining the intensity of subsequent looting between 1989 and 1992). The burial ground included a partly sunken vaulted mudbrick mausoleum with mudbrick tombs and funerary jars. At the heart of the administrative quarter lay a massive palace, with private apartments in one corner and a treasury on the western side.

Three temples and two funerary monuments were excavated, and one of these at the heart of the city displayed a stela inscribed in Greek with a long list of maxims embodying the ideals of Greek life. These were copied from Delphi by Clearchus of Soli, a student of Aristotle, and ended with:

> In childhood, learn good manners; in youth, control your passions; in middle age, practise justice; in old age, be of good council; in death, have no regrets.

Other buildings include a gymnasium with a dedication to the Classical gods Hermes and Herakles, as well as a theatre seating 6,000 where spectators were seated according to their social status; the plan resembles that of a Greek theatre excavated at Babylon. Although the gymnasium and theatre are Greek, as are most of the decorative features, the corridored plans of the palace, temples and houses are inspired by older Achaemenid or local traditions. Additionally, some of the objects, such as a bronze wall-plaque found in the 'Temple of Niches', are either Achaemenid heirlooms or are heavily influenced by earlier traditions. Moreover, the layout of the streets did not follow the idealized model of the regular grid-like blocks espoused by the ancient Greek architect, mathematician and philosopher Hippodamus (498–408 BC). The city therefore represents a fusion of building principles, using local resources to construct 'foreign' features.

Ai Khanum was probably not an isolated experiment of Greek urban planning but evidence to prove this remains to be discovered elsewhere. Extensive investigations at Balkh (which was known as Bactra in classical times), for example, failed to find evidence of this period until the recent discoveries of Greco-Bactrian column fragments and Corinthian and Ionic capitals at nearby Tepe Zargaran (literally, 'Hill of the Goldsmith') raised hopes that this may be the site of the long-lost Hellenistic city. Further evidence for the penetration of Hellenistic building principles comes from excavations at Merv in neighbouring Turkmenistan. This Achaemenid city-site was re-founded not by Alexander the Great, but by the Seleucid king Antiochus I Soter (281–261 BC), and was known in Seleucid times as Antioch Margiana. The older settlement was incorporated by Antiochus into a huge, almost square, defensive circuit measuring some two kilometres across with a rectangular city stretching between the east and west gates. The Seleucid levels are now deeply buried beneath continuous later Greco-Bactrian, Parthian, Sasanian and early Islamic occupation, and have therefore not been explored. Nevertheless, the original fortification walls have been discovered and partly exposed. They were built to a height of ten metres and had a thick solid base rising from a massive platform, supporting a row of vaulted rooms, probably with archers' slits in front, and opening onto an access wall walk behind, the whole thing surmounted by an open crenellated wall walk along the crest. The proportion and design of these defences differ from those at Ai Khanum, but closely resemble Hellenistic stone defences in Turkey, and they probably represent the translation of an imported concept into a more readily available building material. The fortifications were soon reinforced, however, when it was realized that the elegant yet flimsy design rendered them vulnerable to assault using stone-throwing machines.

Whether Seleucid, Greco-Bactrian or early Parthian, the material culture of Alexander's eastern successors was essentially Hellenistic. The finds from Ai Khanum include the lathe-turned ivory leg of a couch that resembles others found in a royal banqueting house later converted into a strongroom at the early Parthian capital at Old Nysa. The source of ivory for both is surely Indian, as was that used for a collection of huge drinking-horns also found at Nysa and which some scholars have suggested are Greco-Bactrian rather than Parthian. Some of the contents of the palace treasury at Ai Khanum probably represent booty seized by the Greco-Bactrian ruler Eucratides while campaigning south of the Hindu Kush. These items include the subsequently scattered remains belonging to a throne encrusted with rock crystal and agate identical to one found at Rome, and an inlaid shell disc probably illustrating an Indian myth. However, imports that might indicate long-distance trade are scarce, although this in itself is noteworthy because it suggests that Parthia may have isolated this Greco-Bactrian kingdom from the West.

Several other objects found at Ai Khanum are purely Hellenistic. Hemispherical sun-dials, inkwells and millstones are of Greek design and the pottery includes distinctive shapes inspired by Western models, including *amphorae*, 'fish plates' and various types of bowl. Moreover, there is evidence for a high standard of carving of stone sculpture. Examples include a carved limestone pillar with the portrait of a bearded man representing the head of the gymnasium where it was excavated, a funerary relief showing a standing youth wearing a short cape clasped at the shoulder (*chlamys*), with his sombrero-like hat (*petasus*) slung on his back to reveal his flowing locks, and a possible statue of the classical Greek god Zeus. A small bronze statuette of a bearded Herakles holding a club and placing a wreath on his own head may be of local manufacture, but other items illustrate continuity of local or the fusion of different artistic traditions. These include terracotta figurines of a jewellery-laden goddess, bone statuettes of a nude female figure and a unique gilt-silver disc representing the Greek goddess of nature, Cybele, standing in an Achaemenid-style chariot within a scene of open-air worship, with priests in Oriental dress. It is likely that, as in the Kushan times that followed or in Parthian Iran, Greek or other deities were identified with older, local gods. Although many of the colonists were Greek, bore names such as Callisthenes and Strato and either came from western Turkey – like king Euthydemus himself – or from northern Greece, others were from local families. Names on inscriptions and graffiti indicate Bactrian residents with Iranian names such as Oumanes, Xatranos and Arixares and prove that some (such as Oxybazos, Oxeboakes, Aryandes) even served as officials in the palace treasury .

Silver coin of Diodotus. Bactria, Afghanistan, c.250–230 BC. British Museum, 1888,1208.66.

Less is known archaeologically about southern Afghanistan during this period of the Greek colonies but four Greek inscriptions have been found at or near Old Kandahar. The first three date to the third century: one is a votive inscription by the son of Aristonax, whose family are addressed in two further inscriptions that are copies of an imperial edict inscribed by the Mauryan emperor Ashoka (r. 268–237 BC). A fourth inscription was discovered recently and is an acrostic poem in Greek dedicated to an individual with the Indian name of Sophytos and which, judging by the content, had originally been set up at his tomb.

Excavations at Old Kandahar during the 1970s by the short-lived British Institute of Afghan Studies revealed Hellenistic defences but little recognizable material of this period within. However, the site equates to the ancient city of Alexandria in Arachosia and a chance discovery from construction outside the old city shows there was a Hellenistic cemetery nearby. Finds included a bronze coffin and two silver and glazed pottery jars (the latter imported from southern Iraq). The jars, with gold wreaths imitating twisted leaf diadems wrapped around them, had been reused as funerary urns containing cremations.

Silver coin of Eucratides I, king of Bactria. Minted in Bactria, Afghanistan, 174–145 BC. Diam. 3.3 cm. British Museum, IOC.24.

Analysis of the distribution of archaeological sites in the hinterland of Ai Khanum shows that it was agriculturally well developed, but only slightly more intensively settled than it had been under the Achaemenids and there is little firm evidence as to the types of crops being grown. This is also true of sites in eastern Bactria, although a series of small forts appear to have been founded by the Greeks on river crossings or fords. Deliberate attention to the surveillance of people moving across such strategic points is underlined by the foundations of fortresses at Kampyr Tepe and Termez on the opposite bank and commanding important crossings of the Amu Darya.

In any case the frontier defences proved inadequate. As described previously, the excavators believe that the city of Ai

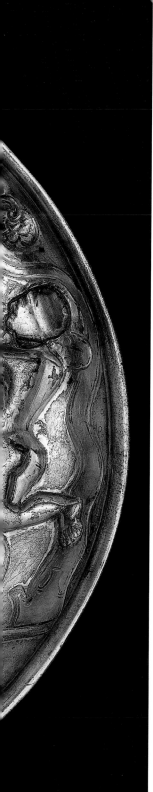

Khanum was destroyed as part of northern nomad incursions into Bactria in 145–144 BC. There is evidence for limited and short-lived reoccupation, until the city was destroyed a second time and abandoned in about 130 BC. The balance between settled and nomadic communities had clearly tipped in favour of the latter. The earlier fear expressed by the Greco-Bactrian ruler Euthydemus during his peace negotiations with Antiochus was finally confirmed. According to the Greek historian Polybius (*c*.200–118 BC):

> [Euthydemus] *invited Antiochus not to refuse to grant him the title and the status of king, given that if he did not comply with his demands, there would be no security for either of them: there were indeed vast hordes of nomads threatening them both, who would be bound to drag the country down into barbarism, if they were allowed to enter it.*

The period that follows shows how the nomad successors to the Hellenistic kingdoms developed their own distinctive culture, which nevertheless included a legacy of their forebears in the continuing use of Greek language.

The design on this bowl is inspired by a late Hellenistic composition of a seated Dionysos being drawn in a triumphal chariot by two Psychai but the metal-working techniques suggest a later date, probably in the 2nd or early 3rd century. It was acquired in Kunduz in 1838 and is one of the earliest finds of silver plate to have been made in this region. Diam. 22.5 cm. British Museum, 1900,0209.2.

Chapter 4

From Indo-Scythians to Kushans:
The Absorption of the Northern Nomads

This striking leaded bronze sculpture was found in the Helmand valley before the First World War (1914–1918) and probably dates to about the 1st century AD. Its wing was crudely repaired at a much later date when a Persian inscription was added, possibly dated to the year 832 in the Muslim calendar (AD 1428/29). H. 24.9 cm; L. 32 cm. British Museum, 1913,1022.1, donated by The Art Fund.

During the second century BC there were several major nomadic incursions into northern Afghanistan. Independent western and eastern historical sources tell us that the successive waves belonged to different tribes who are described as the Asii or Asiani (also given in error as Pasiani), Sakarauli or Saraucae and Tokhari, (the last of whom survive in the later name of the region, Tukharistan, given by Islamic writers), Sai, Kangju (centred on Chach in the Tashkent region of Uzbekistan) and Da Yuezhi (Great Yuezhi). This last group is said to have originated between Dunhuang (in what is now China's Gansu province) and the Tien Shan mountains, but was driven west after a defeat by the Xiongnu, a powerful nomadic empire arising from central Mongolia.

Slate lid of a square cosmetic box decorated with a reclining Bactrian camel. Excavated at Dilbat in southern Iraq, it dates between the 4th and 1st century BC and was probably imported from Afghanistan. 7.1 x 8.3 cm. British Museum, 1881,1103.1896.

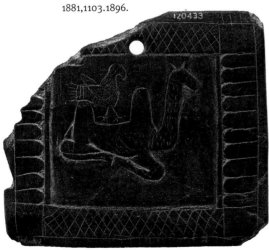

Although they seem confusing at first, these sources actually appear to correlate quite closely. The Sakas were a branch of the Scythians (see p. 38), and may correspond to the Sai described by Chinese writers. According to Justin, they were displaced by the Asii, who are probably to be identified with the later Alans and Ases, and who originated on the western Central Asian steppe before later migrating westwards towards the northern Black Sea.

The Asii are said to have scored a temporary victory over the Tokhari or Da Yuezhi, but the latter are also said to have driven the Sakas out of the Pamirs (an extension of the Himalayas). The Parthians blocked the Sakas from going west into Iran so they occupied southern Afghanistan instead, which then became known as Sakastan ('land of the Sakas'). Some moved further east into the Indus Valley, and a king called Maues ruled northern Pakistan from Taxila, striking coins with Greek and Kharoshthi legends. Others moved into the lower Indus, where by the second century the classical geographer Ptolemy (*c.* AD 90–168) located the land of Indo-Scythia. In the meantime, a new dynasty of Indo-Parthian rulers rose in southern Afghanistan during the first century and briefly supplanted the Indo-Scythians in neighbouring Pakistan, but they were soon to be challenged by another group known as the Kushans.

According to Chinese sources, the Da Yuezhi was divided into five *hsi-hou* (equated with the *yabghu* or governor-generalships of later Turkic tribes) and one of these was called Kushan. They were unified by the Kushan ruler Kujula Kadphises (r. *c.* AD 40–90), and the Kushans went on to establish their rule over a large area extending from Bactria into northern Pakistan, where they ousted the Indo-Parthian rulers who otherwise continued to rule southern Afghanistan. The Greek legacy, however, remained strong. The best evidence for this is the fact that Greek was used on the first Kushan coins struck by Kujula Kadphises and by his successors until about AD 127, and Greek script was adopted to write the local Bactrian language.

The coins of Kujula Kadphises were followed by a series that refer to an unnamed ruler as 'Soter Megas' ('Great Saviour') and 'king of kings'. These coins are found from northern Bactria to northern India and, although anonymous, probably belong to Kujula's successor Vima Takto (r. *c.*90–113), who is described in a Kushan inscription from southern Afghanistan as 'king of kings, the great salvation, Vima Takto the Kushan, the righteous, the just'. In any case they were followed by coins minted by Vima Kadphises (r. *c.*113–27) who reformed the coinage with the introduction of a new copper tetradrachm and gold dinar. He represented himself on the

Copper coin of Kujula Kadphises. The obverse shows a bust of Kujula Kadphises, in the guise of Roman Emperor, facing right. The reverse shows the king, seated on a Roman curule chair, wearing nomadic dress and sword, and extending his right hand. Pakistan, AD 30–80. Diam. 1.8 cm. British Museum, 1850,0305.184.

obverse in the form of a bust, seated or riding a chariot or elephant, with what has been identified by some scholars as the Indian deity Shiva on the reverse (see below).

Vima was succeeded by Kanishka I, whose dates have excited a considerable amount of academic debate but who is now regarded by many as having reigned c.127–50. A monumental inscription found at Rabatak (near the Kushan temple site of Surkh Kotal in northern Afghanistan, then southern Bactria) begins with a description of Kanishka as 'the great salvation, the righteous, the just, the autocrat worthy of divine worship, who has obtained the kingship from Nana and from all the gods, who has inaugurated the year one as the gods pleased'. While Kanishka continues to show himself on coinage in Central Asian dress he stands with one hand over a small fire altar (see opposite), and he introduces a variety of different deities – mostly Iranian and labelled – on the reverse. This dual break with past Greek and Indian traditions reinforces an important shift towards Iranian culture.

The homeland of the so-called 'great Kushan' empire lay in Bactria, and Bactrian continued to be spoken and written in Greek script until the eighth century, when it began to be replaced by Arabic. Our main source of information on the Bactrian language comes from the

Gold coin of Vima Kadphises. India, c.110–127. Diam. 2 cm. British Museum, 1894,0506.4.

study of leather scrolls that began to appear on the art market in 1991, which enabled them to be properly deciphered by the philologist Nicholas Sims-Williams. Places mentioned in these documents suggest that the source of many of these scrolls was north of Bamiyan near the town of Rui, although it is sad that there is no archaeological verification of their findspot. The contents of some of these scrolls are discussed in the next chapter.

The extent of the Kushans' political influence has sometimes been exaggerated, and has been distorted by modern political appropriation by some Soviet and Indian scholars. The archaeological distribution of coins and other material culture does not support claims that Kushan rule extended as far north as Khorezm (south of the Aral Sea), Sogdiana or even Merv – the former two regions were independent, and coin finds prove that the mint at Merv was Parthian. Moreover, excavations of earlier fortifications sealing the northern pass known as the 'Iron Gates' – which controlled a key route between Bactria and Sogdiana in ancient times – indicate that the Kushans rebuilt the Greco-Bactrian defences against northern raiders in the first century AD, to form the northern border of the Kushan empire. A reattribution of mural reliefs decorating a palace at Khalchayan in present-day southern Uzbekistan (previously thought to date to the second or first century BC) suggests they may commemorate a victory by the Kushan ruler Kujula Kadphises over his western neighbours, the nomadic Kangju, who controlled Sogdiana.

Nevertheless, Kushan rule did extend eastwards from Bactria to the lowland plains of Gandhara, the Punjab and what is now northern India. The Kushans became a powerful eastern rival of

Gold coin of Kanishka I, c.127–150. This was part of a hoard found near Peshawar. Diam. 1.9 cm. British Museum, 1879,0501.4, donated by the Punjab Government.

Bronze four-sided Kushan seal from Bagram, showing (from left to right) the deities Oesho/Shiva, Oesho and Umma(?)/Parvati, a Kushan worshipping at a fire-altar and Herakles. *c.* 4th–3rd century BC. H. 1.1 cm. British Museum, 1880.4073, collected by Charles Masson.

Parthia, controlling a natural gateway to and from Central Asia with a route into eastern China, open to Indian cultural and religious influences and an indirect market for Roman luxury items reaching the north-west Indian ports of Barbarikon and Barygaza. Roman commerce with these – along with other ports along the Red Sea and around the Indian Ocean – is itemized in the mid-first century *Periplus of the Erythraean Sea* which goes on to describe them in some detail:

> *Vessels moor at Barbarikon, but all the cargoes are taken up the river* [Indus] *to the king at the metropolis. In this port of trade there is a market for: clothing, with no adornment in good quantity, of printed fabric in limited quantity; multicoloured textiles;* chrysolithon [a golden-coloured gem, perhaps peridot]; *coral; storax* [a resin used as incense and a drug]; *frankincense; glassware; silverware; money; wine, limited quantity. As return cargo it offers:* costus [probably a drug based on a herb from Kashmir]; *bdellium* [a highly sought after aromatic gum resin which was sometimes adulterated with almonds]; lykion [a drug]; *nard* [a plant product originating on the slopes of the Himalayas];

turquoise [from north-east Iran]; *lapis lazuli* [from Badakhshan]; *Chinese pelts, cloth, and yarn; indigo. Those who sail with the Indian* [winds] *leave around July . . . There is in this region* [of Barygaza] *towards the east a city called Ozênê, the former seat of a royal court, from which everything that contributes to the region's prosperity, including what contributes to trade with us, is brought down to Barygaza: onyx, agate; Indian garments of cotton; garments of* molochinon *[mallow-cloth]; and a considerable amount of cloth of ordinary quality. Through this region there is also brought down from the upper areas the nard that comes by way of Proklais (the Kattyburinê, Patropapigê, and Kabalitê), the nard that comes through the adjacent part of Skythia, and costus and bdellium. In this port of trade there is a market for: wine, principally Italian but also Laodicean and Arabian; copper, tin, and lead; coral and* chrysolithon; *all kinds of clothing with no adornment or of printed fabric; multicoloured girdles, eighteen inches wide; storax; yellow sweet clover; raw glass; realgar* [used as a pigment and a medicine]; *sulphide of antimony* [used as cosmetic]; *Roman money, gold and silver, which commands an exchange at some profit against the local currency; unguent, inexpensive and in limited quantity. For the king there was imported in those times precious silverware, slave musicians, beautiful girls for concubinage, fine wine; expensive clothing with no adornment, and choice unguent. This area exports: nard; costus; bdellium; ivory; onyx; agate; lykion; cotton cloth of all kinds; Chinese* [silk] *cloth;* molochinon *cloth;* [silk] *yarn; long pepper; and items brought here from the* [nearby] *ports of trade.*

Gandharan bronze reliquary from Wardak (known as the Wardak Vase), containing Kushan bronze coins of Vima Kadphises (*c.* AD 113–172), Kanishka I (*c.* AD 127–150) and Huvishka (*c.* AD 150–190). Excavated by Charles Masson in 1835. H. 17.6 cm. British Museum, 1880.93.

The *Periplus* continues by stating that beyond Barygaza lay 'several tribes' and 'above these is the very warlike nation of the Baktrianoi, who are under their own king', a reference to the Kushans. Archaeological evidence provides a good deal of information on the Kushans. The discoveries in two hidden strongrooms at the heart of what is possibly the Kushan royal summer palace of Kapisa (near modern Bagram) are particularly revealing, providing a glimpse into Afghanistan's importance in the complicated network of trade routes that connected India with Central Asia. Bagram lies next to the confluence of the rivers Ghorband and Panjshir, and commands the junction of two major roads to Bactria – one to Balkh through the Bamiyan valley and the Shibar pass and the other to Kunduz over the Khwak pass. The rooms in question were decorated with wall-paintings and lined with brick benches and were found with the doors deliberately bricked up and plastered over in order to conceal the contents beyond. Excavated in 1937 and 1939, they were found to be piled high with objects. Many were in very poor condition, and even the total number remains unclear. They included Indian wooden furniture decorated with over a thousand carved and painted ivory and bone plaques secured with metal rivets; some fifty plaster type casts for reproducing multiple copies in metal showing elements from Classical Roman mythology; about 180 glass vessels (mostly from Roman Egypt); bronze tablewares; carved and polished rock crystal; alabaster and porphyry vessels, again from Egypt; ostrich eggs mounted as *rhyta* (wine-pourers) and hundreds of Chinese painted lacquer bowls. Perhaps originally there were other items, too, such as tablecloths or soft furnishings, which did not survive.

These finds were at first interpreted as warehouses for Silk Road trade as that was one of the key areas of interest of the French archaeological mission to Afghanistan. The excavator, Carl Hackin, initially believed them to date from the first to early fourth

The Bimaran Reliquary. Inset with stones and containing gold staters of Sabina (c. AD 128– 136), Vima Kadphises, Kanishka I and Huvishka. Excavated by Charles Masson in 1833/34. H. 6.5 cm; diam. 6 cm. British Museum, 1900,0209.1.

centuries AD, although this wide date-range was later narrowed to the first or possibly early second century, thus only a little later than the *Periplus*. The location of the rooms within the heart of a palace rather than a bazaar warehouse suggests that they are in fact the hoarded wealth of a local ruler reliant on gift exchange and ostentatious display to emphasize his status.

Another barometer of economic development during this period comes from archaeological surveys and excavations in areas of northern Afghanistan. Although Ai Khanum was abandoned (see p. 57) and the number of sites in eastern Bactria declined by more than 50 per cent, northern and probably central Bactria enjoyed a peaceful period of economic development and continuity of settlement. Moreover, the modest Greco-Bactrian foundation at Old Termez (then in northern Bactria, now Uzbekistan) was massively expanded in size, its citadel was doubled and new fortifications established consisting of a hollow curtain wall with rectangular projecting towers. The growth of this fortified settlement on the banks of the Amu Darya reflects its position directly opposite the city of Balkh on the route ultimately connecting India with Samarkand, and it dominates the Surkhandarya valley. This valley was intensively developed, and archaeological surveys show a tenfold increase in settlements during the Kushan period. Dalverzin Tepe, also in northern Bactria, grew from a small Hellenistic fort to a walled town measuring 720 by 570 metres across, with streets laid out on a grid; excavations there have revealed a small palace, a number of temples (including a Buddhist shrine with statuary) and a potters' quarter. The unexcavated fortified settlement of Shahr-i Nao on the upper Surkhandarya reached a staggering 350 hectares, surrounded by seven kilometres of defences. Other towns such as Dilberjin Tepe and Zar Tepe functioned as smaller, new administrative centres at the heart of rural districts. These typically possessed a square citadel overlooking a fortified rectangular or square town.

In many cases careful attention was paid to ensuring a good water supply. The first large Bactrian inscription to be discovered was in a Kushan temple at Surkh Kotal and it refers to how a local administrator called Nokonzok (who is also mentioned in the Rabatak inscription) restored the security of the temple and ensured its water supply:

> *He walled the acropolis, then he dug this well and led out its water and fitted stones to it, so that to the men in their acropolis water should not be lacking and* [so that] *when they have fear of enemies then they remove not the gods from the seat and abandon not the acropolis. And over the well he built a waterwheel,* [and he] *installed a tank, so that by means of this well, by means of this waterwheel the whole acropolis fare well.*

The well in question was constructed at the foot of a monumental terraced staircase leading up to a temple with a square inner sanctuary surrounded by a corridor. The decoration is eclectic and includes stepped battlements, a Gandharan stone frieze, and a series of painted clay and carved stone representations of Kushan kings. The complex was at first identified as a Zoroastrian fire temple but although its location fits Strabo's description of the Iranian religious custom of offering 'sacrifice on a high place' (*Geography* XV, iii.13), the identification of the religious ceremonies is uncertain.

Other religions were practised across the Kushan kingdom too and it was during this period that Buddhism spread from the Indian lowlands across much of Afghanistan. There are two types of

Buddhist religious monument: cave monasteries and monasteries built of stone and/or brick with prominent stupas (dome-shaped constructions containing relics). The greatest concentration of these in Afghanistan is in the Kabul valley near the ancient city of Bagram. The stupas were richly decorated with clay sculptures, and occasionally imported representations carved in the distinctive style developed in the neighbouring Gandhara region of northern Pakistan, which used soft local grey stone to great effect and combined elements of Classical Roman and Indian art.

The secular arts found at Kushan sites in Bactria are similar to contemporary Parthian and Central Asian styles, and made use of polychrome painted clay or stucco sculpture and wall paintings. The colour palette is a continuation of Hellenistic tradition, with pink, yellow, green and blue added to the traditional red, brown, black and white. Entirely new, however, was a shift to frontal depiction, with figures depicted in native horse-riding dress of belted tunic worn over trousers. The Roman author Dio Chrysostom (c.40–c.112) recognized this innovation: he wrote how the Bactrians 'were among the finest masters of the art of horse-riding' and that 'the foreigners attired themselves according to their custom, wearing a turban and trousers for the Persians, the Bactrians and the Parthians'. The first-century victory murals at Khalchayan (mentioned on p. 63) add further details; they depict a horseman firing his bow, the hoof of a horse trampling armour and another figure carrying armour as a trophy. The caricatured enemies compare closely with depictions on carved bone plates found in a Kangju grave at Orlat in Uzbekistan, and now dated to the first or second century. A small number of clay figurines from other sites also appear to depict armoured warriors.

Little is known about the relationship between the Kushans and their northern nomadic neighbours but archaeological finds suggest there was trade. Glazed pendants made in Roman Egypt and traded via the western Indian Ocean were moved north and west through Kushan territory, then deeper into Central Asia where they were probably exchanged for local trinkets. The route runs through north-west Afghanistan, and it is here that some spectacular archaeological evidence was discovered at the archaeological site of Tillya Tepe (literally 'Hill of Gold') in 1978. The treasure discovered here, which includes more than 20,000 gold ornaments and other items, has become popularly known as the 'Bactrian Treasure'.

During the first century, the summit of a long-deserted site was transformed into a small elite cemetery consisting of a male grave surrounded by five (possibly originally six) equally spaced female graves, all interred with fantastic personal wealth. The graves can be dated from the evidence of the associated imported Chinese mirrors, Roman glass and coins. The latter seem to have been placed either in the mouth or held in the hand of the dead, and were conceivably intended as a local version of the classical practice whereby the dead needed to pay Charon, the ferryman to the Underworld. This custom began to spread across the Middle East from the first century onwards, but what exactly the mourners at Tillya Tepe intended is unclear. Later Muslim instances of this practice, for example, reveal that the payment was meant for Munkar and Nakir, the interrogatory black-faced blue-eyed angels of death, during the first night of interment, and in recent times in the Bahia oasis of the Egyptian Western Desert, people still occasionally placed a coin in the mouths of the elderly to prevent other deaths in the family.

Each of the bodies at Tillya Tepe was buried fully dressed, judging by the remains of belts, scabbards and thousands of tiny gold appliqués originally sewn onto cloth (sadly the textiles

Grey steatite reliquary with coins. Made in Gandhara, Pakistan, 1st–3rd century; found in Kotpur in Afghanistan. H. (with lid) 7.4 cm; diam. (of body) 10.3 cm. British Museum, 1880.96.

themselves do not survive). The exact style of dress – or even whether some were shrouds rather than clothing – has attracted several different theories. Similar debate surrounds some of the jewellery. Some is purely classical and some might be heirloom booty seized from Greco-Bactrian treasuries; however, the frequency of turquoise inlays is a feature of northern nomad production, and there is a surprising scarcity of local Badakhshan-sourced stones such as lapis lazuli or garnet. Some deep blue inlays are actually glass rather than stone and this is again a feature of some nomad production and suggests that the makers did not have access to the Kushan controlled mines. Other finds point to multiple routes of trade: there is a miniature lion amulet carved from amber, either from the Baltic or Mongolia; a set of beads partly made of what is probably jet, for which the nearest source is in north-east Iran; and pearls that must come from the Persian Gulf or India. Some of the

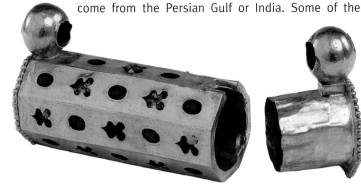

Gold octagonal amulet box, inset with stones. Made in Gandhara, Pakistan, 2nd–3rd century; found at Ahin Posh near Jalalabad, Afghanistan. L. 7.4 cm; w. 3 cm. British Museum, 1880.29.

pieces show signs of partial loss, wear and repair, indicating that they had been worn or used before burial.

The identity of the dead is unknown. Some scholars have suggested that they belonged to a newly settled community occupying a nearby site at Emchi Tepe, who reused the deserted mound at Tillya Tepe as a place of burial because it reminded them of the type of barrow (*kurgan*) they used to build on the steppe. However, this site is of a different period and it is more likely that the graves belong to a nomad elite. A similar phenomenon has been discovered more recently at Kok-Tepe in Uzbekistan, where a woman was interred in an old site, and placed on a couch while wearing gold-ornamented clothing with a beaded veil and diadem, a Chinese mirror and comb placed in an embroidered bag, smouldering incense-burners at her head and feet,

Fragment of a Roman marble sarcophagus carved in relief with the scene of the Indian triumph of Bacchus, conqueror of the East. Probably from Phrygia in west central Turkey, *c.* AD 300. 76.5 x 70 cm. British Museum, 1973,0327.42.

and the remains of a funerary feast stacked up outside. A series of similar high-status burials have also been found in an arc extending north-westwards through the Central Asian steppe as far as the Black Sea. They belong to what is termed the Sarmato-Alan civilization. The graves at Tillya Tepe therefore should no longer be regarded as Da Yuezhi or Kushan as the excavator proposed, nor are they royal, but are most likely to be the tombs of a local tribal

Sketch of Bamiyan by the explorer Charles Masson (a name he used as an alias after deserting from the British East India Company army) who visited the site in September 1832. It shows the Western Buddha on the left, the smaller Eastern Buddha in the centre and some of the many grottoes cut into the cliff-face around. Pencil on paper. The British Library Board.

chief and his family. They open an exceptional window into the consumption of imports by nomads and the rich visual appearance of the ornaments attached to and worn with their textiles (although we have little idea of their colours or possible embroidery which would have created a colourful visual complement to the art of the goldsmith).

The last of the so-called 'great Kushans' was Vasudeva I (c.190–230). At the end of his reign, northern Afghanistan was invaded by the Sasanians and the Kushans lost their northern territories although they continued to rule in southern Afghanistan, Pakistan and India. Afghanistan had flourished under the previous two centuries of Kushan rule and had been part of a powerful kingdom that extended across northern Pakistan to north-west India. This provided the mechanism by which Buddhism was spread westwards and northwards into China by missionaries, and also explains the large numbers of Indian, Chinese and Roman items (imported via India) in the palace at Bagram.

Chapter 5

Interactions with Sasanian Iran:

Kushan-shahs, Huns, Hephthalites and Turks

Kushano-Sasanian silver plate showing an investiture scene. The surfaces are heavily smoothed from repeated rubbing in ancient times and parts of the separately made relief decoration are missing, as is the left hand portion, probably because these were melted down for reuse of the silver. 4th century. Diam. 24.6 cm. British Museum, 1897,1231.188, bequeathed by Sir Augustus Wollaston Franks.

Between the early third and mid-fourth centuries, and again briefly during the fifth century, Afghanistan was part of the Sasanian Empire; at other times it was ruled by successive waves of Central Asian nomads who entered the country from the north. There were strong cultural influences from Iran and India, as well as a heavy Buddhist presence with considerable investment in monasteries and the construction of the famous colossal Buddhas of Bamiyan. The strength of belief in Buddhism helps explain its survival and partial revival during the first centuries after the Islamic conquest.

This scene is from a cave in Ghulbiyan, northern Afghanistan. It shows a king in Sasanian dress with a queen and courtiers paying homage to Zoroastrian deities. Probably 4th century. Drawing by Ann Searight based on photos taken by Jonathan Lee.

In AD 224, an Iranian nobleman from Istakhr – near Persepolis, the ceremonial capital of the former Achaemenid Empire, in southern Iran – overthrew his Parthian overlord Artabanus V (r. c.213–224) and crowned himself king in the capital of Ctesiphon in present-day Iraq. This ruler was Ardashir I (r. c.224–40), founder of the new Sasanian dynasty which created a strong empire lasting for more than four centuries until the

Arab conquest in the seventh century. This empire developed a
wealthy economy with a highly developed agricultural system,
tolerant integration of different ethnic and religious minorities
including Christians, Jews and Buddhists, and a powerful
professional army which not only maintained the empire's border
defences but regularly defeated Roman armies during periodic
clashes between these two empires.

In the initial stages of building his empire, having consolidated
his hold on Iran and Mesopotamia, Ardashir began to extend his
rule eastwards. The oasis-city of Merv appears to have been taken
later, when he is said to have killed 'a large number of people'
whose heads were allegedly sent to a temple of the Iranian
goddess Anahita. For a brief period an autonomous local ruler

The large Buddha at
Bamiyan, with the remains
of later fortifications on
the right. Lithograph with
hand-colouring; print by
J. Lowes Dickinson, 1843,
after a drawing made by
Lieutenant Vincent Eyre
who was held hostage
there in 1842 after the
British retreat from Kabul
earlier that year. 10.1 x
16.1 cm. British Museum,
1970,0527.2.28, donated
by Miss M. W. MacEwen.

Bamiyan valley with the colossal Buddhas at the rear. Photo: Bill Woodburn.

issued his own coinage at Merv, with a princely bust on one side and a horseman on the other, and inscribed 'mrwy MLK' ('Merv king'). This individual may be the same as another Ardashir who is described as ruling during the reign of Ardashir I in the later inscription of Shapur I (r. 240–72), which was added to the exterior of an older monument at the royal ceremonial site of Naqsh-i Rustam, near Persepolis, in 262. This also makes it clear that by this date all Afghanistan was firmly within the Sasanian Empire:

> the state of Shapur I, 'shahanshah of Iran and non-Iran', included Varkan [Gurgan], Merv, Harev [Herat], the whole of Abarshahr, Kerman, Segistan [Sistan], Turan [near Kalat in Baluchistan], Makuran [Makran], Paradan [near Quetta], Hindustan [Sind], Kushanshahr up to Pushkabur [Peshawar]

and up to the boundaries of Kash [Kashgar], *Sughd*
[Sogdiana] *and Shash* [Tashkent].

Merv was probably a springboard for the Sasanian army under
Ardashir I to take Bactria. Southern Afghanistan was occupied
shortly afterwards under Shapur I and for the following 150 years
Afghanistan was part of the Sasanian Empire, ruled either directly
or through governors called Kushan-shahs ('kings of the Kushans').
Often Sasanian princes, they continued to issue coins with Bactrian
inscriptions, using a more cursive form of the script than
previously. A dramatic illustration of how Sasanian control was
commemorated was discovered by the British anthropologist
Jonathan Lee in 2001 near Pul-i Khumri in northern Afghanistan: the
face of a cliff overlooking an important pass connecting Bactria
with the Kabul region was found to be carved with the relief of a
Sasanian king, probably Shapur I, hunting rhinoceros. These are
hardly local to the region and the scene was intended to
symbolize domination over India.

Carnelian ring bezel showing the portrait busts of a bearded man wearing a diadem and a lady wearing a crown. An inscription at the top is in Sogdian and states 'This seal is of (or from) Indamič, Queen of Začanta.' Kushano-Sasanian, 4th century. L. 3.3 cm. British Museum, 1870,1210.3.

The best corresponding evidence for everyday
life during Kushano-Sasanian times comes from
excavations of a residential quarter at Zar Tepe
(pp. 68–9) in northern Bactria (present-day
Uzbekistan). The finds included pottery which
continued the earlier local Kushan tradition of
streak-burnished red-slipped wares which were
probably inspired by the visual effect of metal
equivalents, but there are some new forms too.
These include open bowls with rims that curve
inward and which resemble a shape seen in
Sasanian and locally produced Kushano-Sasanian
silver bowls. Other features shared by Kushano-Sasanian

and Sasanian material culture include bone hairpins and horse figurines supporting bowl-shaped incense-burners, while other imports include Indian cowries, shell bangles and Roman glass. The last doubtless inspired the addition of lions' heads to local pottery, as this type of decoration was common on contemporary Roman glassware and a complete Roman cut-glass bowl with lion-headed appliqués has been found in a grave in a burial ground at Dzhalpak-Dyobyo (modern Kyrgyzstan). Another new ceramic form typical of objects found from this period is a deep bowl with wavy handles and incised decoration on the inner surface of the outward-curving rim. An imported Roman type of metal bowl with swinging handles probably inspired this form. Local potters copied examples of these not only in Bactria, but also in the neighbouring Merv oasis. Mould-made fired clay figurines belong to a much older, local tradition, and differ totally from contemporary Sasanian versions from Merv. In both cases, however, they represent popular religious belief and superstition independent of the official faiths of Zoroastrianism or Buddhism.

Above Sasanian ring bezel carved from carnelian and inscribed 'Perozhormizd, son of the Kanarang' in Middle-Persian (*Pahlavi*). It refers to a powerful general governing the north-east frontier of the Sasanian Empire. 3rd century. L. 3.1 cm. British Museum, 1966,0723.1.

Right Sasanian personal seal carved from lapis lazuli. The design shows a lion with a scorpion above and a star and crescent below. An inscription in Middle-Persian reads 'Reliance on the gods.' *c.* 5th century. Diam. 1.7 cm. British Museum, 1846,0523.379.

Zoroastrianism was now the official religion of Iran but – despite the impression given by brief periods of orthodox proclamation – many other faiths were also practised across the Sasanian Empire.

In Afghanistan this was a

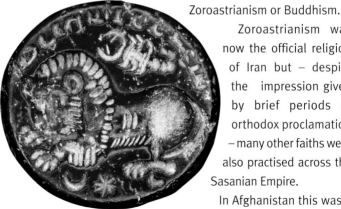

boom period for Buddhism as large numbers of monasteries were founded, and it was probably through familiarity and free movement that Buddhism entered the Sasanian Empire from Bactria: two Buddhist monasteries are known at Merv, and a piece of Gandharan sculpture was excavated as far west as Veh Ardashir, the twin city of Ctesiphon. Other beliefs appear to be manifested in burial customs. Kushano-Sasanian and later Hephthalite burials excavated at sites such as Kandahar were found with Sasanian silver drachms placed in the mouths of the deceased, recalling the practice seen earlier at Tillya Tepe in northern Afghanistan and reflecting popular superstition rather than orthodox religious belief (p. 71).

Chalcedony stamp-seal engraved with a contest scene between the hero Rustam, wearing Iranian dress and brandishing a bull-headed mace, and a child-devouring demon with wild hair and straggling beard. From Afghanistan, 4th century. Diam. 2.7 cm. British Museum, 1905,0530.1.

Evidence for seasonal occupation of caves, probably by pastoralist tribesmen, has been found at archaeological sites near the village of Aq Kupruk in northern Afghanistan's Balkh province and at Shamshir Ghar Cave in Kandahar province in the south. A cemetery excavated at the neighbouring site of Said Qala Tepe may even represent that cave's occupants. Another small cemetery, possibly fifth or sixth century, was found inside a cave at Aq Kupruk; the excavated graves contained red burnished pottery, a bronze mirror, iron weapons and horse trappings, a silver ring with a lapis lazuli setting and various beads of carnelian and lapis lazuli.

Sasanian control of Afghanistan ended in the mid-fourth century following another massive nomad invasion from the Altai region to the north. In ancient times, authors gave these invaders different names, and there has been much debate over exactly who they

were and their ethnic and political relationships. They are variously called Chionites (in Latin sources), Kidarites (by Greek authors), Honk (Armenian literature), the Ta Yuezhi or Lesser Yuezhi (Chinese annals) and grouped together with the Hephthalites in Indian literature as the Huna. However described, they were an eastern branch of the Huns which was a powerful tribal confederation extending westwards through southern Russia. According to the

contemporary Roman author Ammianus Marcellinus, the Sasanian emperor Shapur II marched against them in 346/7, but following a peace treaty they sent troops to take part in his siege of the eastern Roman fortress of Amida (modern Diyarbakir in Turkey) in 359. The Kidarites established a capital near Balkh and, according to the later Chinese chronicle *Pei-shih* (Annals of the Wei Dynasty), written in 643, they conquered Gandhara and other territories

Hephthalite silver bowl depicting a hunting scene. 5th century, said to have been found near the river Swat in the North-West Frontier Province of Pakistan. British Museum, 1963,1210.1, given by Max Bonn.

south of the Hindu Kush. The same source states that they 'move around following their herds of cattle' yet they were not purely nomadic and not only settled but also struck gold, silver and copper coins and battled the Gupta rulers of India for control of the Punjab. Coins give inscriptions in Sogdian, Bactrian, Middle Persian and Brahmi but it is not known what language the Kidarites spoke, nor is there much information about their history.

Around the mid-fifth century another Hunnic group of tribes known as the Hephthalites replaced the Kidarites in northern Afghanistan. The sixth-century Byzantine historian Procopius (500–65) described them as follows:

> The Ephtalitae are of the stock of the Huns in fact as well as in name; however, they do not mingle with any of the Huns known to us, for they occupy a land neither adjoining nor even very near to them; but their territory lies immediately to the north of Persia; indeed their city, called Gorgo, is located over against the Persian frontier, and is consequently the centre of frequent contests concerning boundary lines between the two peoples. For they are not nomads like the other Hunnic peoples, but for a long period have been established in a goodly land.

The Hephthalites proved to be a dangerous threat to Iran, and the Sasanian king Peroz (r. 457–84) campaigned against them twice, once being captured and ransomed, and the second time losing his life. According to Priscus, a fifth-century Byzantine chronicler, 'the cause of [the war] was that the Huns were not receiving the tribute monies which the former rulers of the Persians and the Parthians had paid'. At this time the Sasanians strengthened their eastern defences, building a long wall with an

outer ditch running over two hundred kilometres from the Kopet
Dagh mountain range on what is now the frontier between Iran and
Turkmenistan to the Caspian Sea, with an extension or second wall
returning south from the Caspian to the Elburz mountain range, to
enclose the entire Gurgan region of north-east Iran.

The Bactrian leather scrolls mentioned previously (p. 63) add
some economic details of life in Afghanistan under the Kushano-
Sasanian, Hun, Turkic and finally Arab overlords. Many are letters;
others are legal contracts including slave sales, leases,
guarantees, receipts and deeds of gift or release of slaves, and
prices are usually given in gold dinars or Sasanian silver drachms
(and later Arab dirhams). They refer to places within the
jurisdiction of an otherwise unknown local ruler called the '*khar* of
Rob': Rob is identified as modern Rui, on the Khulm river north of
the Hindu Kush. Many were rolled and sealed with lumps of clay,
known as *bullae*, impressed with the personal seals of witnesses,
and include references to the local gods Ram and Vaksh (the
deified river Oxus). Less is known about everyday material culture
of this period, but personal seals suggest strong Sasanian
influence on the iconography, and versions of Sasanian winged
crowns are depicted on locally produced terracotta figurines in
domestic contexts and probably used in household ceremonies.
Moreover, wall-paintings from Dilberjin near Balkh and Balalyk-
Tepe show armed men wearing kaftans and scenes of feasting with
men in the company of women and drinking from stemmed metal
goblets. Hunting and feasting are also celebrated on silverwares.

The Chinese writer Sung Yün stated that most Hephthalites 'do
not believe in Buddhism' and instead honoured 'foreign gods',
including a 'heaven god' and a 'fire god'. Chinese sources refer to
a variety of burial customs such as 'if a man dies, a wealthy family
will pile up stones to form a house [over the body]; a poor family

will dig the ground for burial. The articles of everyday use are buried with the dead'. Another source refers to how 'the coffin is laid in a wooden case'. There is some archaeological evidence to support these statements as excavations at Shakh Tepe, near Kunduz, revealed a Hephthalite cemetery.

Buddhism continued to flourish in Afghanistan in the fifth to eighth centuries. The most famous monument is the monastery complex at Bamiyan, where two enormous standing figures of Buddha, 38 and 55 metres high respectively, were largely carved from the living rock, the details and projecting forearms originally modelled with painted clay and stucco on a wooden armature. A combination of recent radiocarbon dates on the wood and detailed art-historical study now suggest a mid-sixth century date for the smaller Eastern Buddha and an early seventh century date for the larger Western Buddha, both somewhat later than originally supposed. The surrounding cliff face is honeycombed with hundreds of small monastic cells, hostels and storerooms. Both the colossal sculptures and many of the grottoes contain extensive traces of polychrome murals, partly influenced by Indian, Sasanian and Hun art, and new scientific analyses reveal the use of many pigments including ultramarine (crushed lapis lazuli). These monumental remains attracted the attention of many later travellers, including the Chinese Hsüan-tsang (c.602–64), who visited between 629 and 632 and described the larger Buddha thus: 'On the declivity of the hill to the north-east of the capital was a standing image of Buddha made of stone, 140 or 150 feet high, of a brilliant golden colour and resplendent with ornamentation of precious substances.' The great fourteenth-century Syrian geographer Yaqut describes both, remarking on a chamber supported by columns high up on the mountain side, its walls carved with representations of 'every species of bird that Allah had

Opposite This carved steatite lid of a cosmetic box is probably of the Hephthalite period and possibly early 6th century, judging by the style of portraiture of the lady. H. 6.8 cm; w. 6.1 cm. British Museum, 1920,0517.1.

created – most wonderful to see', while outside were 'two mighty idols cut in the live rock of the hill-side, from base to summit, and these are known as the Surkh Bud and the Khing Bud [the Red and Grey Buddha] and nowhere else in the world is there aught to equal these.'

The size of the Buddhist monuments at Bamiyan indicates a high degree of religious donation, reflecting the physical location of this valley. It functioned as one of the main passes connecting Balkh with the Indus via Kabul, and grew wealthy from passing trade. This explains the medieval Arab geographer al-Muqaddasi (c.945–c.1000) calling it 'the trade-port of Khurasan and the treasure-house of Sind', while the Iranian chronicler of the Ghurid dynasty, al-Juzjani (980–1037) says that its rulers:

> . . . have been famous and celebrated upon all occasions from the most remote ages for the grandeur of their station, the abundance of their riches, the vastness of their treasures, the number of their mines, and their buried wealth . . . That tract of country has also been famed and celebrated to the utmost parts of the countries of the world for its mines of gold, silver, rubies and crystal, garnets and other [precious] things.

The chronology of many other monasteries is less certain, but those at Tepe Maranjan near Kabul, Fundukistan, Tepe Shotor ('Camel's Mound'), Tepe Sardar and Basawal are likely to date to this phase, as do cave complexes at Kakrak, Foladi and Dukhtar-i Nushirvan. The current rescue excavations of monasteries at Mes Aynak, in the copper-rich Logar valley south of Kabul, should provide important new evidence on the development of Buddhist art during this period, as vividly painted stone sculptures and a wooden representation of Buddha are the first such finds to be

made in the country. However, the largest concentration of Buddhist monasteries is in the Hadda area of the Jalalabad valley connecting Kabul with northern Pakistan, where the ruins cover some 15 square kilometres and are said to include more than a thousand stupas. Buddhists considered this valley one of the most sacred places, and Chinese travel accounts dating to 420, 520 and 632 state that Buddha received his inspiration here. They also list various stupas as marking the spot where he shaved his head and pared his fingernails, or containing relics including a tooth, his robe and his staff. The earliest of these Buddhist pilgrims, Fa-hsien (337–c.422), begins his description thus:

> *In the city of Hiro* ['bone'] *there is a shrine which contains Buddha's skull-bone, entirely covered with gold-leaf and ornamented with the seven preciosities* [gold, silver, lapis lazuli, rock-crystal, carnelian, coral, ruby]. *The king of the country deeply venerates the skull-bone; and fearing lest it should be stolen, has appointed eight men of the leading families in the kingdom to hold each of them a seal, with which to seal and guard the shrine and bone . . . Every morning the king makes offerings and worships in this manner, afterwards transacting affairs of State . . . In front of the gate to the shrine there will be found, regularly every morning, sellers of flowers and incense, so that all who wish to make offerings may buy of all kinds. The kings of the countries around about also regularly send envoys . . .*

Hephthalite rule in northern Afghanistan ended in the mid-sixth century with the expansion of a Turkic tribal confederation from the Central Asian steppe. Between 563 and 567, the Turks routed the Hephthalites near Bukhara (in what is now Uzbekistan) and displaced them into the Chaganian region of Central Asia, where according to Arab accounts they lingered until the Arab Conquest in the eighth century. Local rulers appear to have acknowledged Turk supremacy and became vassals of the kaghan but the political situation remained tense: the Sasanians took Balkh in 588/9 and killed the Turk kaghan in battle but a few years later the Sasanian governor of Khurasan was murdered by Parmowk, the vassal ruler of Balkh, and – according to a later Arab account – parts of Iran were briefly overrun in 616/7 by a Turkic army.

In the meantime, during the later fifth, sixth and early seventh centuries, the region south of the Hindu Kush had been ruled by local Hun dynasts, some of whom took the title of Khinghil but who mostly bore Indian names and struck coins using the Brahmi alphabet. One of these, Narendra II, appears to have ruled the area extending from Kabul to Kashmir during the late sixth and early seventh centuries; his son Yudhishthira appears to have been overthrown by the Kashmiri Karota dynasty. He was replaced by Turkish rulers known as the Türk Shahi dynasty who controlled the Kabul–Gandhara region until the ninth century. At this time of local rule we see the construction of small forts with circular corner towers, such as at Bagram, and the production of a distinctive type of pottery jar decorated with medallion-like stamps showing portrait busts and other designs. Buddhism continued to flourish under these rulers but discoveries of Hindu marble sculptures also indicate the spread of other Indian religions, and Sasanian-style seal portraits with Brahmi inscriptions attest cultural assimilation. There is evidence too for the immigration of a Turkic population settling in Gandhara, Kapisa and Zabulistan and also references to the *avagana* (Afghans) in the Indian *Brhat-samhita*, mirrored by Hsüan-tsang's account of crossing the land of A-p'o-k'ien (derived from *Avagan*) while travelling back to India.

Chapter 6

Medieval Islamic Dynasties

Brass jug decorated
with silver inlays.
c.1200. H. 15.3 cm.
British Museum,
1885,0711.1a.

The Arab conquest of the Sasanian Empire, including what is now Afghanistan, was neither quick nor easy. It began with border raids in Iraq during the early seventh century. These grew in number and success as the Sasanian ruling class, army and economy were weakened by decades of war on multiple fronts and political intrigue within the court itself. As the Arab armies became emboldened and strengthened by deserting Sasanian troops bringing their own equipment, they began to move in further. Sasanian cities were heavily defended and the usual tactic was therefore to offer terms of surrender, rather than engage in costly and risky sieges.

After almost two decades the Arab forces reached the eastern frontier at the oasis-city of Merv, where the fleeing Sasanian king Yazdigird III (r. 632–51) had finally taken refuge. The governor surrendered, and Yazdigird was murdered on his orders in AD 651. Once again (and not for the last time), Merv became a springboard for military intervention, in this case for Arab armies entering northern Afghanistan and Central Asia, where they clashed with Turks, Tibetans and Chinese.

In 653 the first raids were made on Balkh in northern Afghanistan,

View of the late medieval fortifications of Balkh. These had been restored by Timur (1335–1405) and were described in 1404 by a visiting Spanish ambassador as 'a broad rampart of earth which along the top measures thirty paces across'. Photo: Bill Woodburn.

and a second Arab army commanded by Abbad ibn Ziyad entered Helmand in the south-west via Sistan. According to the ninth-century historian al-Baladhuri, he 'crossed the desert until he came to Kandahar', which was then renamed Abbadiya, either after its conqueror or because of the 'high turbans of the natives'. The slightly uneasy status quo is reflected in the terms of the peace treaty described by the Iranian historian al-Tabari (839–923), whereby both parties agreed that 'the desert regions . . . should be out of bounds [to the Arabs]. When the latter went out anywhere, they would warn each other for fear they encroach on any of [these regions] and so break the peace.' The Arab hold of these newly conquered areas continued to be tenuous however and the area

Remains of the early Islamic mosque at No Gumbad in Balkh. The lower portions of the decorated columns are buried in earth. Recent excavations suggest this mosque may have been founded as early as the 8th century. Photo: Bill Woodburn.

Detail of the carved stucco decoration at No Gumbad. This may have been originally painted in bright colours although no traces of this remain. The monument is now protected by a roof and is being carefully restored. Photo: Alison Gascoigne.

south of the Hindu Kush was contested by a local dynasty. The penetration of Islamic belief was equally slow and Buddhism remained dominant until the eighth century.

In 736 Balkh (formerly known as Bactra) finally succeeded Merv as the capital of Khurasan, Iran's major north-east province. The ninth-century geographer Yaqubi refers to it having a 'gate of the Indians' (*bab-al Hinduwa*) and a 'gate of the Jews' (*bab-al Yahud*), and the anonymous tenth-century Persian author of *Hudud al-alam* attests its many bazaars. The latter work also contains one of the earliest explicit references to Afghans, in a place somewhere near Gardez, east of Ghazni: 'Saul, a pleasant village on a mountain. In it live Afghans.' The contemporary Arab geographer al-Muqaddasi (*c*.945–*c*.1000) quoted another Iranian source stating that 'Balkh is brilliant' and praised the 'excellence of its situation, the width of its roads, the splendour of its streets'. The city was particularly famous for its produce. Al-Muqaddasi listed 'soap; sesame; rice; walnuts; almonds; raisins; dried grapes; clarified butter; honey of grapes dried in the sun; figs; pomegranates; vitriol; sulphur; lead; *asbark* [a herb]; arsenic; armour like that made in Jurjan [north-east Iran]; garments; oil and fats; and skins'. His contemporary, the Iranian author Tha'alibi (961–1038), added that 'its specialities include garnets, the neuphar or waterlily [the roots of which were eaten], soap and many other things I am unable to mention here'. An important silversmiths' quarter with its own mosque is attested from the eleventh century, doubtless exploiting the fact that Balkh was the administrative centre for the silver mines of the Panjshir valley. Lapis lazuli continued to be mined and cut into bezels for finger rings, or crushed as pigment for wall paintings and ceramics.

Medieval writers describe other distinctive products of Afghanistan which were traded across the region. Many were dried or processed foodstuffs, including raisins, syrups and preserves. The Basra-born scholar al-Jahiz (*c.776–c.868*) singled out the 'good grapes and mushrooms' of the Balkh region. Soaps and asafoetida were traded locally, and various types of cheese and clarified butter, horns, furs and fox skins were traded across northern Afghanistan. As in other parts of the Islamic world, textiles also feature prominently although many of these industries were probably much older than these first references suggest. Weaving was a major industry of Kunduz according to al-Mustawfi (*c.1281–c.1340*); the geographer ibn Hawqal (943–969) refers to the settlement of az-Zalikan, one day's journey from Bost, as being dominated by weavers; cotton textiles (*karbas*) were produced at Bost; and carpets, hangings, rugs and covers are described as among the products of the region of Sistan. Salt was the chief export of the town of Rudhbar in Sistan. Writing in the ninth and tenth centuries, Yaqubi and al-Muqaddasi state that Kabul was a major exporter of certain dried fruits and astringent nuts used in medicine (which were described in medieval sources as 'myrobalan'). This city is also said to have possessed numerous warehouses for indigo, Indian

Silver coin minted in northern Afghanistan *c.*894–902 by Abu Da'ud Muhammad ibn Ahmad (r. 874–898 or 899) and excavated at the Persian Gulf port of Siraf. Diam. 2.2 cm. British Museum, 2009,4088.28.

and Chinese cloth, and separate quarters where Muslims, Jews and Buddhists lived. Al-Muqaddasi also refers to the manufacture of woven date-palm frond baskets, palm-fibre rope and reed mats in Sistan, and Tha'alibi adds 'drinking bowls, bells for hawks, drums for ceremonial occasions and silk brocade hangings and coverings' to the list. The same author refers to inflatable skins, apples,

rhubarb and a buttermilk drink as specialities of Ghazni. Steel was produced in Herat, almost certainly using the same crucible technology as archaeologically demonstrated from the same period at Merv. Gold, horses, mules, felts, carpets, saddlecloths and cushions were exported from the mountainous area of Gharj-ash-Shar, and asbestos was mined in the north in Badakhshan for using as long-lasting lamp wicks and woven table covers that, according to al-Muqaddasi, could be oven-baked to remove the grease.

During the ninth century Afghanistan broke apart during the power struggles of the Abbasid caliphate, and the different regions became virtually independent of the Abbasid capital of Baghdad. Parts of the northern region remained within the province of Khurasan which was ruled by the Tahirids from their capital at Nishapur in north-east Iran. The Balkh area was governed by a local dynasty known only from its coins and named after its founder Abu Dawud Muhammad as the Abu Dawudids. South of the Hindu Kush, Sistan was seized by one Yaqub ibn Laith al-

Opposite Minaret of Bahram Shah ibn Mas'ud (r. 1117–*c*.1157) at Ghazni: this was the work of the last Ghaznavid ruler and the city was sacked in 1151 by the Ghurid ruler Ali al-Din. The relief decoration is in unglazed brickwork; the upper part is missing and has been replaced by the modern conical cover. Photo: Getty Images.

Left Detail of the carved brick decoration and inscription on the 12th century Seljuk minaret at Dawlatabad near Balkh. The Seljuks were a powerful turkish tribe (discussed further on p. 110). Photo: Alison Gascoigne.

Saffar (r. 840–79), who founded a new dynasty known as the Saffarids. Little is known of him other than his name, which literally means the 'coppersmith'. The *Tarikh-i Sistan* (*Book of Sistan*), anonymously written in the mid-fourteenth century, refers to his father being of the same trade, and thus both must have been well-known in the bazaar and key players in the local economy. Yaqub made Zarang (modern Nad-i Ali, just inside the Afghan border with Iran) his capital. Tenth-century geographers describe it as a circular city, including a citadel, a town with five iron-clad gates and separately fortified suburbs, with three kilometres of markets and shops extending from the Mina Gate (literally, 'port') which may have been on a canal, as the city boasted its similarity to Baghdad on the river Tigris. Water supply was channelled by canal from the Helmand river and distributed to individual properties, which included sunken rooms to shelter from the scorching summers. Sadly, little is visible today and medieval writers refer to the humid climate rotting the timbers and exposing them to insects. The

Opposite The famous Ghurid minaret at Jam, the second highest minaret in the world after the Qutb al-Minar in Delhi which was inspired by it (for further discussion, see p. 110). H. 63 m. Photo: David Thomas.

region is notorious for its *bad-i-sad-o-bist-ruz* ('wind of 120 days'), which blows forcefully from June to September leaving many sites sand-blasted.

The subsequent two-century history of the region is described in the *Tarikh-i Sistan*. Yaqub took control of the Kabul region in 871 and overthrew the Tahirid rulers of Khurasan two years later. His success led an Iranian poet from Qom in Iran to compare him with Alexander the Great; the later Baghdadi historian and geographer al-Mas'udi (*c*.896–956) described how Yaqub sent presents to the caliphal court in Baghdad in 896:

Below Carved marble wall-panels lining the courtyard of the palace of Mas'ud III (r. 1099–1114), at Ghazni. Photo: IsIAO.

Noteworthy among them were a hundred Mehri camels from Khurasan, a great number of dromedaries, many chests of precious materials and 4,000,000 dirhams. There was also a brass idol representing a woman. She had four arms and was wearing two silver belts embellished with red and white stones. In front of this idol there were other smaller ones, whose arms and faces were decorated with gold and jewels. The idol was placed in a wagon specially fitted out for them, drawn by dromedaries . . . The people nicknamed the idol Shughl – 'A Hard Day's Work' – *because everyone stopped what they were doing to go and see it during the days it was on view.*

Doubtless this was captured booty from a Hindu temple. The respect Yaqub was owed by his troops, again according to al-Mas'udi, 'leaves far

Small square and polygonal monochrome glazed ceramic tiles excavated in a Ghurid residence at Ghazni are decorated with single animals and plants enclosed in a beaded border reminiscent of the pearl roundels on Sasanian and later art. c.1150–1215. British Museum, 2003,1205.1, donated by E. Roesdahl.

behind everything we are told on this subject of the kings of antiquity', but after Yaqub's death his brother and successor Amr failed to hold Khurasan and it fell to the Samanid governors of Transoxiana, while Kabulistan regained its former independence.

The ninth century also witnessed the rise in power of Turkish slave troops among the native Iranian Samanids, as well as at the Abbasid court in Iraq. Alptegin, one of the Turkish generals, moved from Bukhara to Ghazni, about 145 kilometres south-west of Kabul, and founded his own military base there in 962. This was to become the capital of a new Muslim dynasty known as the Ghaznavids. Mahmud ibn Sabuktakin (r. 998–1030), popularly known as the 'Idol-smasher', led the occupation of former Samanid territories up to the Amu Darya valley. His reign marked the apogee in the fortunes of the Ghaznavid Empire; followed by his son Mas'ud I (r. 1030–41), he not only campaigned across the Amu Darya but also into Iran and north-west India where he sacked the famous sun temple at Somnath in Rajasthan, a shrine to the Hindu god Shiva, in 1025. In recognition, the Abbasid caliph al-Qadir (r. 1031–75) gave him the title *yamin al-dawlah wa amin al-millah* ('Right Arm of the State and Trustee of Islam'). Huge quantities of booty, including precious metals, jewels, slaves and trophies, were brought back from Rajasthan, and excavations in Ghazni revealed a large statue of the Hindu god Brahma set as the threshold of a mosque, the face worn smooth by the regular passage of feet.

Mahmud was a major patron of Persian literature. His court is said to have included 900 scholars and 400 poets, including the Iranian scholar al-Biruni (973–1048) and the poet Abdul-Qarim Firdausi (*c.*925–1020) who dedicated his epic *Shah-Nama* ('Book of Kings') to Mahmud. However, in the absence of the rich reward he expected, Firdausi changed it to a satire and fled back to Iran. A first-hand account by one Abu al-Abbas al-Tusi describes his impressions of Ghazni when he took a message to Mahmud from the Abbasid caliph al-Qadir (r. 991–1031):

> *When I reached the outskirts of the city where he resided, I came across a large number of troops, far more than I had ever seen, in the best attire and outfit and the most complete armour and equipment. Then I entered the city where the army was mobilized. After that I came to an enormous number of elephants surrounded by – so I was told – thirty thousand men from India. I passed by them and saw a great number of young Turkish slave soldiers living in the palace rooms, all with armour and weapons, and I was told there were some ten thousand . . . when I reached Mahmud, I found him gorgeously decked out in an enormous audience hall, which was highly decorated and well equipped. He was seated on a throne, and the leaders of his kingdom were standing before him in two rows in the finest and most beautiful attire.*

French excavations at Lashkari Bazaar, near modern Lashkar Gah in southern Afghanistan, revealed a sprawling complex of palaces, villas, gardens and barracks constructed by Mas'ud I and overlooking the river Helmand. The reception rooms were richly decorated with figural wall paintings and geometric carved plasterwork. A later palace at Ghazni belonging to Mas'ud III

Pottery jar with applied and stamped decoration, and small inset spots of turquoise glaze. Said to be from Maiwand, north of Kandahar, *c*. 12th century. British Museum, 1978,1012.1, donated by Mr M. J. W. English.

(r. 1099–114), known as the 'Beneficent Sultan', was subsequently investigated by an Italian archaeological expedition. The huge central courtyard was paved with marble and faced with polychrome painted plaster and elaborately carved marble friezes with interlaced geometric decoration and scenes of courtly life, hunting and animal combat. Related designs, including elephant riders, lute players and mounted falconers, are represented on mould-pressed coloured glass roundels some 5–10 centimetres across. Some twenty of these were excavated in a palace of the Ghaznavid ruler Bahram Shah ibn Mas'ud (r. 1117–*c*.1157) at Old Termez, and others are reported from Ghazni itself. These were presumably set into window grilles, and al-Muqaddasi commented on how the wooden buildings in Ghazni were 'set [with] what is called *ghashak* resembling the tessellation of Egypt'. The wealth of the court is illustrated by a passage in a chronicle entitled *Kitab Zayn al-Akhbar* (*Book of the Ornament of Histories*) completed by the Iranian geographer Gardizi in about 1048, which describes a banquet hosted by Mahmud to impress Qadar Khan, the Qarakhanid ruler of Ma-wara-n Nahr (Transoxiana):

Brass ewer with lightly engraved roundels decorating the body. Islamic, *c*. 12th century. H. 23 cm. British Museum, 1992,0714.2.

It had been splendidly laid out, with extraordinary sweet-smelling flowers, delicious fruits, gems, a dinner service of gold and silver, crystal ware, mirrors and other rare things. Qadar Khan stared at it all. They sat together for a while. Qadar Khan did not have wine: it is not customary for the Kings of Ma-wara-n Nahr to have wine, particularly not the King of the Turks among them. They listened to music for some time, and stood up. Then Prince Mahmud, may God grant him compassion, ordered a gift to be prepared of gold and silver utensils, costly gems, Baghdad filigree, fine fabrics ... to be given to Qadar Khan as a mark of honour and generosity.

Brass lamp-stand, 11th century. Glazed pottery versions of these are also reported from Afghanistan. H. 75 cm. British Museum, 1954,0216.1, donated by P. T. Brooke Sewell, Esq.

The same author also details camel trappings decorated with silver bridles and lunar discs, while the Khurasani poet and philosopher Nasir-i Khusrau (1004–88) mentions seeing 'two large silver door rings' on the door of the Kaaba at Mecca c.1050, which he says were sent from Ghazni. This implies that there was a thriving metal industry in Ghazni, one that included goldsmiths and silversmiths. Few of these precious items survive as it was customary to melt them down when necessary, and at times there was a puritanical backlash against consumption of luxury materials. The *Tarikh-i Sistan* describes how two secretaries of the treasury struck gold and silver coins in about December 985 because: 'No gold and silver was left in the treasury. It had all been used or given away. They began to sell off vessels, and to strike [silver] dirhams and [gold] dinars from the gold plate, *zarrine*, and silver plate, *simine*.'

Less expensive metalwares do survive in some quantity however. Jugs, ewers, bowls, basins, flat dishes, stands, shallow rectangular trays, lamps, tripod-footed lamp-stands, hollow incense-burners in the form of birds or lynxes, rosewater sprinklers, mortars, inkwells and pen cases have been found at archaeological sites in places such as Ghazni, Lashkari Bazaar, Kandahar and Maimana (in northern Afghanistan near the Turkmenistan border). Some were hammered from sheet copper and were strictly functional; others were cast from brass and were more elaborately decorated, sometimes with silver inlays. High-tin bronze was also used to make lamps and jugs. All are part of a wider eastern Iranian tradition, often described as Khurasani. Some may even be traded products

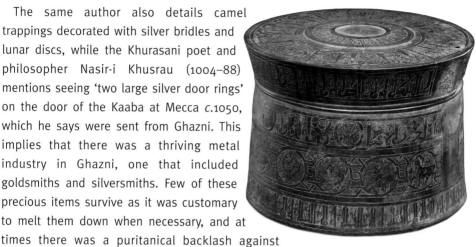

Lidded brass box with inlaid gold and silver decoration. Khurasan, 12th century. Diam. 23.5 cm. Lathe-turned painted wooden boxes of this shape were also made in Afghanistan. British Museum, 1967,0724.1, funded by Brooke Sewell Permanent Fund.

or spoil from Merv, Nishapur, Herat or Transoxiana as few are signed, all were mass-produced and many of the external parallels are from the art market rather than archaeological contexts.

Afghanistan was part of an equally broad ceramic tradition stretching from eastern Iran deep into Central Asia: the most distinctive types include serving bowls covered with white slip and decorated on the inside with colourful slip-painted designs which were covered with transparent glaze to protect them during regular cleaning. These were mass-produced and archaeological evidence suggests that there were many different workshops. Less is known about other craft industries, but the manufacture and working of glass, either for vessels or windows, was widely diffused through Iran and Central Asia by this period.

In 1040 Ghaznavid fortunes began to fail when Mas'ud I was decisively defeated in the battle of Dandanqan by a former Turkish client tribe from the lower Jaxartes (Syr Darya). These were the Seljuks who went on to found their own powerful empire, occupying Baghdad in 1055. The Seljuks failed to take Ghazni, however, and peace was maintained for another century. In 1151, after growing hostility between the Ghaznavids and a family dynasty from Ghur, the mountainous region east of Herat that the Ghaznavids had never succeeded in taking, the Ghaznavid capital was sacked by Ali al-Din Husain (r. 1149–61). Thousands were killed, others deported as forced labour, libraries set on fire and most of the Ghaznavid royal tombs broken into and the contents exhumed and burnt.

The Ghurids now replaced the Ghaznavids as the dominant dynasty in Afghanistan. They were acknowledged as such by the Saffarids of Sistan, and the later Ghaznavid rulers were forced to retreat into the Punjab. Ghurid power reached its highest point under the rule of two brothers, Shams al-Din or Ghiyath al-Din

Brass jug with
silver inlay showing
astrological symbols.
Herat, c.1200. H. 40 cm.
British Museum,
1848,0805.2.

(r. *c.* 1163–1203) of Ghur and Shihab al-Din, also known as Muizz al-Din (r. 1173–1203), of Ghazni: whereas the former kept the Khwarezm-shahs at bay to the north, the latter regularly campaigned into India. It was during this period that the world's tallest minaret, the Qutb al-Minar, was built in Delhi, directly inspired by the spectacular 63-metre high minaret constructed in the heart of the Ghorat mountains at Jam, in north-west Afghanistan's Ghor province (pictured on p. 102). Kufic inscriptions winding around the exterior of this give the entire text of the 19th Sura of the Qur'an (which ends with a promise of the pleasures of the Garden of Eden for true believers) and state its construction by Ghiyath al-Din, 'Sultan Magnificent! King of Kings!'. It probably belongs to the fabled Ghurid summer capital of Firuzkuh ('Turquoise Mountain'). According to al-Mustawfi, Herat grew wealthy in this period; with 12,000 shops, 6,000 hot baths, 659 colleges and a population of 444,000 and after a fire, Ghiyath al-Din rebuilt its Great Mosque in 1200. Other monuments of this period include a masonry-built mosque at Larwand, near the southern border of the Ghurid kingdom in the central Afghan mountains. Constructed in north-west Indian style, it was presumably designed and built by architects and masons from that region who had been converted to Islam. Stone and brick castles and watchtowers illustrate a reference by the geographer Yaqut (1179–1129) to the numerous strongholds of these rulers, and help to explain their success against their Ghaznavid predecessors and the difficulties they later posed to the Mongols.

Less is known about everyday Ghurid arts and crafts but archaeological excavations at Ghazni, Lashkari Bazaar, Bamiyan and Jam indicate the types of ceramic vessel in use. There is evidence for the import of lustreware, enamel-painted *mina'i* ware and underglaze-painted pottery from Iran as well as Northern Song

Opposite Cast brass flask or bottle with a pair of handles in the form of goats. Engraved with blessings and inlaid with silver. *c.*1200. Acquired in the Punjab and possibly made in the Indian provinces of the Ghurid Empire. H. 31.4 cm. British Museum, 1883,1019.7.

dynasty celadon-glazed porcelain from China. Local regional traditions produced varieties of stonepaste wares covered with turquoise glaze (so-called 'Bamiyan fritwares'), plain and incised glazed pottery, unglazed relief-moulded pottery jugs and handmade wares, often painted in black with bold geometric designs. As with metalwork produced in the preceding Ghaznavid period, many of these classes of pottery belong to a wider tradition uniting eastern Iran and Central Asia.

The thirteenth-century Iranian cosmographer Zakariyya al-

Opposite The *Masjid-i Jumi'* ('Friday mosque') at Herat. Founded in the early Islamic period, it has been heavily rebuilt and restored over the succeeding centuries. Photo: Alison Gascoigne.

Below Detail of the tilework on the dome of the mausoleum of Gawharshad Begum, wife of the Timurid ruler Shah Rukh (1377–1447), at Herat. Photo: Alison Gascoigne.

Qazvini claims Herat was central to an export trade of inlaid brass work and some surviving metal vessels bear the signatures of their makers. Their quality was very high, and this is illustrated by the so-called 'Bobrinski bucket' in St Petersburg's Hermitage Museum, which is covered with figural friezes depicting musicians, revellers, huntsmen and backgammon players, highlighted through the combination of brass, copper and silver to create a clear and polychromatic effect. Dated to the equivalent of December 1163, it carries the following inscription:

> *Ordered by 'Abd al-Rahman ibn 'Abdallah al-Rashidi, made by Muhammad ibn 'Abd al-Wahid, worked by hajib Mas'ud ibn Ahmad the decorator of Herat, for its owner the brilliant khwaja Rukn al-Din, pride of the merchants, the most trustworthy of the faithful, grace of the pilgrimage and the two shrines, Rashid al-Din 'Azizi ibn Abu al-Husain al-Zanjani, may his glory last.*

Ghur was the Ghurid capital and was an important centre for armour production. The local historian al-Juzjani states that the ruler Izz al-Din (r. *c*.1145–*c*.1163) supplied the Seljuk ruler Sultan Sanjar (r. 1118–57) every year with 'such things as had been customary and established [in previous times], such as breast-plates, coats-of-mail, helmets, and other war materials', but these supplies were later withheld by Ali al-Din in about 1149. Other anecdotes supplied by this writer provide rare evidence for the appearance of early Islamic armour and indicate that the Ghurids wore long mail shirts covered with coloured surcoats, which had to be tied up when they dismounted from their armoured war elephants to fight on foot.

The Ghurid dynasty effectively came to an end in 1206 with the murder of Muizz al-Din as he prepared to avenge an earlier defeat by the rulers of Khwarezm (south of the Aral Sea). These rulers briefly overran the Ghurid kingdom, but their success was short-lived: within fifteen years, the Mongols had conquered all of Central Asia and yet another new power held sway in Afghanistan.

The shrine of Hazrat Ali at Mazar-i Sharif which stands on the site believed to be the tomb of Ali, son-in-law of the Prophet Muhammad and the fourth caliph, who was murdered in 661 in southern Iraq, but whose body was said to have been strapped to a camel which wandered into Afghanistan. Photo: Alison Gascoigne.

Chapter 7

From Mongols to Mughals

Illustration from the *Khamsa of Nizami* manuscript (the 'five poems' of Nizami Ganjavi, a 12th century Persian poet), dated 1494/95. The image depicts various vessels, including a *mashrabah* (brass jug) being carried by the servants. British Library, Or.6810; © The British Library Board.

بدان صورت چه صنعت کرد بلخی
بسر سبزی بر آن سبزه نشستند
عروسانی ز نا شویی ندیدم
بکاوین از جهان خواهم و از ابروان

رسیده دید آن کی روی ای پی
کز آن غنچ طبرزد رخت شدی
کلاپیسه بستند
وزانجا چون پری شد نا بدید
که از نگاه شاخ درختی
به و سانپ بر شاخ درختی

In 1219 the Khwarezmian governor of the city of Otrar (in modern Kazakhstan) made the fatal decision of executing a large mission sent by the Mongol ruler Chinggis (Genghis) Khan (r. 1206–27). He confiscated their property, then executed the delegation sent to demand an apology. The aftermath was swift and terrible and the wave of retribution spread across Central Asia, Afghanistan, Iran and Iraq.

The Mongols sacked Otrar after a five-month siege in which most of the population perished. The city of Bukhara surrendered in the same month, but was still sacked and its able-bodied male population placed at the front of the Mongol assault on Samarkand in a human shield. This city surrendered the following month, but again suffered a brutal punishment. It was thoroughly looted, the Turkish garrison killed and, according to the Chinese traveller Ch'ang Te, its population reduced to 25,000 from 100,000 people. Gurganj (modern Urgench), the capital of Khwarezm, was also sacked after a lengthy siege by three of Chinggis's sons: Jöchi (c.1180–1227), Jagatai (c.1185–1241/2) and Ögödai (c.1186–1241). Its craftsmen, women and children were enslaved, with the remainder of the population divided into batches for convenient slaughter. Hotly pursued by two of Chinggis' best generals, Sultan Muhammad Khwarazm (r. 1200–20) fled to Balkh, then across northern Iran. Balkh was sacked and its population massacred for harbouring their former ruler. According to the medieval geographer ibn Battuta (1304–68/9), who travelled as widely as North Africa and China, Chinggis demolished a third of the columns in Balkh's Great Mosque looking for treasure supposedly buried beneath. The siege of Bamiyan involved the death of the son of Jagatai, Chinggis' grandson, and in revenge Chinggis ordered all living creatures – whether men, women, unborn children or animals – to be exterminated, buildings levelled, a ban enforced on re-settlement and the name of the site changed to Mav Balik (the 'accursed city').

The former eastern Seljuk capital of Merv was besieged in 1221, and when it surrendered its population was marched outside the walls for a three-day period of slaughter. Mongol detachments pursued the Khwarezm-shah through Iran, sacking Nishapur and Tus in turn, until he died of exhaustion on an islet in the Caspian. His son, Jalal ad-Din (r. 1220–31), offered resistance in the Hindu Kush, but was defeated and fled first to India, then Iran, and finally Iraq, where he was murdered in 1231. In the meantime, his headquarters at Ghazni was sacked and the city abandoned.

Medieval writers aghast at this passage of events exaggerated the numbers slaughtered by the Mongols, but they are indicative of the scale of devastation: between 300,000 and 700,000 killed at Merv and 1,600,000 at Herat. The purpose was partly revenge, partly to strike terror and partly to avoid leaving populations that could overwhelm the overstretched Mongol garrisons, but it was also intended to develop new pasturage as an extension of their traditional nomadic economy. Ibn al-Athir described it:

These recently restored defences were built in the early 15th century by the Timurid ruler Shahrukh (1377–1447). New archaeological excavations have revealed earlier medieval fortifications beneath and a new museum has opened inside. Photo: Aga Khan Trust for Culture.

Another detachment turned towards Ghazna and its surrounding area, and moved on into the neighbouring areas of India, to Sistan and Kerman. They behaved here in the same way as their fellows, perhaps even worse. Never had anything like it been heard of. Even Alexander [the Great], who all sources agree in saying was the ruler of the world, did not come to dominate it so rapidly, but needed ten years to do so: he did not kill anyone, but was content with the submission of the people. But in just one year they [the Mongols] seized the most populous, the most beautiful, and the best cultivated part of the earth whose inhabitants excelled in character and urbanity.

View of the exterior of the extensive 15th-century Timurid shrine complex at Gazurgah on the outskirts of Herat. This was built around the tomb of a Sufi Muslim saint, Khoja Abdullah Ansari who died in 1089. Photo: Aga Khan Trust for Culture.

During much of the following century, Afghanistan was left to the devices of local warlords operating beyond the rule of the successors of Hulagu Khan (r. 1256–65). One of these local warlords was Neguder – a former general supported by the survivors of a Mongol force previously commanded by Chinggis' eldest son Jöchi – who held the area around Ghazni. Sistan was ruled by a local dynasty, and from c.1250 until 1383 Herat was governed by the Karts, who claimed descent from the Ghurids.

At the beginning of the fourteenth century, the Karts and the Neguderis were obliged to pay homage to the descendants of Chinggis' second son Jagatai, who ruled Transoxiana. During this period Herat took the former provincial capital role of the oasis-city Merv and grew wealthy on the proceeds of trade between Iran and Central Asia which now bypassed the contested frontier region of Merv. Herat continued to be an important centre for the production of inlaid brasswork, including small cast pot-bellied dragon-handled jugs of standard capacity (800 ml), known as *mashrabahs*. These were often signed with the maker's name and typically inscribed in Persian with verses referring to wine, water or the 'water of life'. The inscription on one in the British Museum begins:

Come, O cupbearer, for the
Beloved has taken off the veil
The work of the lamps of the
recluses are rekindled
That snuffed out candle came
into flames, again
And this old man, advanced in years,
has again become a youth.

Miniature by Ustad Kamal al-Din Bihzad (c.1460–1535), one of the great calligraphers and miniaturists of the Iranian world, showing the construction of the legendary castle of Khawarnaq as an illustration of an epic by Nizami (see p. 118) British Library, Or. 6810; © The British Library Board.

Chinese porcelain and jade vessels with dragon-headed handles pre-date the earliest known brass versions and must be the inspiration for this form, albeit customized for a wider middle-class clientele through the addition of Persian poetry and elaborate inlaid decoration.

Timurid brass jug (*mashrabah*) inscribed in Persian and giving the name of its maker, Muhammad ibn Shans al-Din al Ghuri, and dated to the equivalent of 11 April 1498. Made in Herat. H. 14.2 cm. British Museum, 1962,0718,1.

The Great Mosque in Herat's city centre also contains a famous massive cast bronze cauldron dated 1375, with one inscription from the Qur'an and a second stating that it was presented to the mosque by the local Kart ruler Muhammad ibn Muhammad. Ibn Battuta stayed in Herat when he passed through the region in 1333, before travelling on to Jam, which he describes as 'of middling size in a fertile district. Most of the trees are mulberries, and there is a great deal of silk there.' By contrast, Balkh was 'an utter ruin and uninhabited'; the silver mines at Panjshir had been abandoned since the Mongol sack; 'nothing but a fraction' of Ghazni remained; and he describes Kabul as 'formerly a vast town, the site of which is now occupied by a village inhabited by a tribe of Persians called Afghans. They hold mountains and defiles and possess considerable strength, and are mostly highwaymen.'

The situation changed in 1369 with the rise of Timur, better known as Tamerlane (1335–1405) and founder of the Timurid dynasty. Timur belonged to the Barlas clan of Mongols, and rapidly rose from military governor until he was elected Great Amir after his capture of Balkh in 1370. He made the city of Samarkand (in modern Uzbekistan) his capital and began a wide-ranging series of campaigns. Spoils and craftsmen were sent back to Transoxiana, where they stimulated the local arts and crafts. Ruy González de Clavijo, a Spanish ambassador to Timur's court in 1403–5, remarked that 'wheresoever he went he carried off the best men of the population to people Samarkand, bringing thither together the master craftsmen of all nations'. Timur captured Herat in 1380, removing the city gates and executing the last Kart ruler soon afterwards. He then took Kabul, Ghazni and Kandahar. Sistan resisted, but paid a heavy price, as Timur destroyed one of the great dams on the river Helmand and sacked the capital at Zarang in 1383, slaughtering everyone who could be found and flattening its defences. In 1398 Timur achieved what earlier Mongols had not and sacked Delhi. He went on to besiege Damascus (1401) and Ankara (1402), and died on campaign en route to China in 1405.

After his death, his only surviving son, Shah Rukh (1377–1447), soon took control and ruled until his death in 1447, making his capital at Herat where he had been governor previously, while sending his own son Ulugh Beg (1394–1449) to hold Samarkand. Shah Rukh's priority was to consolidate rather than continue his father's exploits, and he strengthened the defences of Herat. The period that followed was one of the high points of the city. He established the surviving cruciform layout of the bazaars at its heart, with the junction roofed as the *Char suq* ('four bazaars'). Shah Rukh's wife, Gawhar Shad ('Bright Jewel'), commissioned a *madrasa* (place of learning) and *musalla* (place of worship) in 1417, completed in 1432. This complex was largely destroyed in 1885, but a domed mausoleum and two minarets survive. East of Herat is the famous tiled shrine at Gazurgah, which was built around the tomb of the local eleventh-century Sufi poet–philosopher Khwaja Abdullah-i Ansari (b. 1006) and restored by Shah Rukh in 1428.

According to the local contemporary historian Abdulrazzak, his court was a great sight to behold:

*In the royal garden were erected tents, which had from
eighty to a hundred poles, scarlet pavilions, and tents
made of silk. In these tents were thrones of gold and silver,
encircled by garlands of rubies and pearls . . . Bazaars and
shops, richly ornamented, recalled the beauty of the garden
of Irem. Cupolas, fascinating to the eye, elegantly decorated,
seemed like caskets filled with precious stones, or
constellations of numberless stars. Cupbearers, on silver
pedestals, with hands as white as crystal, smiling lips,
and holding golden cups, gave everywhere the signal of
pleasure. Singers sang to melodious tunes the songs
formerly heard at the court of the Sasanians. Skilful
musicians, touching deftly the lute and the lyre, ravished
the reason of the listeners. In each tent was a magnificent
reception room. The diversions were prolonged for many
days without interruption. The Emperor was prodigal to all,
to those of low as well as to those of high rank, of his
generosity and munificence.*

The idea of creating tent cities with movable palaces remarkable
not only for their size but also for their different textures and
colours of cloth was created by the Mongol khans. It is hardly
surprising that Timur and his successors chose to adopt them as
they combined the luxury of the court with a nomadic heritage.

Shah Rukh had three sons: Ibrahim and Baysunghur – both fond
of Persian poetry – and Ulugh Beg, mentioned above and who
famously built an observatory in Samarkand. The creation of
illuminated manuscripts and bookbindings reached a high point
under Timurid court patronage; the most celebrated of these
miniature painters was Bihzad, of whom it was said by Qadi Ahmad
that 'no one had seen an artist equal to him since the art of images

came into being'. Shah Rukh's son Baysunghur himself was famous for preparing a new edition of the tenth-century poet Firdausi's great Persian epic the *Shah Nama* ('Epic of Kings'), which survives in the Gulistan Palace museum in Tehran. These miniatures detail aspects of courtly material culture, many of which do not survive, including geometric interlaced and floral patterned carpets with stylized Kufic inscriptions around the borders, and a wide range of metal bell-shaped candlesticks, trays, cups, ewers and the *mashrabahs* (see p. 124). Unsurprisingly, blue-and-white glazed pottery inspired by, and at times closely following, imported types of Chinese porcelain survives in greater quantity, as does a class of so-called '*Kubachi*' ware (named after a town in the Caucasus where it was first recognized), which is characterized by blue painting under a transparent glaze on an artificial composition body. These, or similar, wares were commented on by a Chinese ambassador, Ch'en Ch'eng, who visited Herat in 1414:

Monument of Babur (1483–1530), the *Chihl Zina* ('forty steps') at Kandahar. An unfinished Persian inscription inside begins 'On the 13th of Shawal 928 H. [1522] the Emperor Babur conquered Kandahar, and in the same year he ordered his son Mohammad Kamran Bahadur, to construct this lofty and splendid building'. It continues with the aspiration that 'Great hopes are entertained that some more of the rich countries will fall into the Emperor's hand.' Photo: Alamy.

The porcelain vessels are extremely fine, and on them are delicately drawn flowers and grass in fine colours. They are extremely beautiful but they do not match the light, blue, clear and sparkling ones of China. If such a vessel is hit, it makes no sound. The nature of clay is like this.

The Baghe Babur in Kabul. Babur's favourite garden included running water, flowers and fruit trees, and was periodically restored by later Mughal rulers. It was restored by Abdur Rahman Khan and remodelled in the 1930s by Nadir Shah who created a more European feel. Badly destroyed in the civil war it has been restored since 2002 by UN-Habitat, Development and Humanitarian Services for Afghanistan and the Aga Khan Trust for Culture. Photo: Aga Khan Trust for Culture.

Shah Rukh sent an embassy to Beijing, with one member commenting wistfully: 'In the arts of stone-cutting, carpentry, pottery, painting, and tile-cutting there is nobody in the whole of these lands who can compare with them.' Another source of information on crafts of this period comes from references to craft guild displays organized on the occasion of particular festivals. Within the Middle East these are best known from the Ottoman period, but the practice began under the Timurids. In 1412/3, Shah Rukh ordered that the Herati bazaar be decorated and each shop be made clearly visible, and in 1448/9 Ala al-Dawla decreed that the Baghe Zaghran in Herat be adorned with 'every craft and art of the craftsman of the seven climes in every fashion that you might wish'. This spectacle was captured in miniature in 1465/6 by one

Khwaja Ali Ardagar Isfahani, who:

> *showed in a rosewater bottle thirty-two types of trades of the*
> *workshops of the world with each trade engaged in its own*
> *speciality. Thirty-two shops and workshops were opened,*
> *and every craftsman was engaged in his own special trade,*
> *and those which necessitated movement in the plying of*
> *their trades, such as tailors, cotton pressers, carpenters, and*
> *ironworkers, were seen to be moving.*

In the mid-fifteenth century there was a succession struggle, but in 1469 Husain Baiqara, a descendant of Timur's son Umar Shaikh, took the throne and restored peace. He rebuilt some of the major buildings in Herat and added a summer pavilion to the Baghe Murad gardens beyond the city walls. He was also responsible for the construction of a new shrine for the supposed tomb of the caliph Ali at Mazar-i Sharif (the 'Noble Tomb'). In Herat, the Great Mosque – previously rebuilt by the Ghurid ruler Ghiyath al-Din in 1200 – was restored by Husain Baiqara's minister Mir Ali Sher Nawai.

At the end of the fifteenth century there was further turmoil in Central Asia as a strong new confederacy of Uzbek tribes became even more powerful. Led by Muhammad Shaibani (*c.*1451–1510), a descendant of Jōchi, they forced the teenage Zahir al-Din Muhammad Babur (1483–1530), the last Timurid prince, to take refuge in the Hindu Kush. Herat was taken by the Uzbeks in 1507, but then lost three years later to Ismail I (1487–1524), founder of the powerful new Safavid dynasty in Iran, and it was to remain outside the control of rulers from Kabul until the late nineteenth century. Babur made Kabul his base, then captured Kandahar, commemorating his achievement in Persian inside the nearby rock-cut monument known as *Chihl Zina* ('Forty Steps'; see p. 127).

His memoirs – the *Baburnama* – underline the importance of these two cities:

> *There are two trade-marts on the land-route between*
> *Hindustan and Khurasan: one is Kabul, the other Kandahar.*
> *Kabul is an excellent trading centre . . . Down to Kabul every*
> *year come seven, eight or ten thousand horses and up to it,*
> *from Hindustan, come every year caravans of ten, fifteen,*
> *twenty thousand heads of houses, bringing slaves, white*
> *cloth, sugar candy, refined and common sugars, and*
> *aromatic roots . . . In Kabul can be had the products of*
> *Khurasan, Rum* [Turkey]*, Iraq and China; while it is*
> *Hindustan's own market.*

Babur went on to invade India and successfully counter elephants and cavalry with cannon and muskets, until then both unheard of in northern India. He took Delhi in 1526 and made it the capital of his Mughal empire. Delhi and Agra were to be his homes from then on, but he continued to love Kabul, fondly referring to an area of gardens along the banks of the river Jumna in Agra as 'Kabul'; and his body was brought back to that city for burial in his favourite garden, the Baghe Babur ('Babur's Gardens').

Babur's memoirs and later Mughal miniatures and poetry stress the importance of the natural landscape. Nur Jahan, the famously beautiful wife of the emperor Jahangir (r. 1605–27), is said to have personally supervised the planting of each tree in the garden at Nimla, some 40 kilometres from Jalalabad in eastern Afghanistan, with alternating cypress and plane trees delineating regular squares planted with narcissus. Rings in the courtyards of the royal city of Fatehpur Sikri in Rajasthan were used to secure the ropes of elaborate marquees, which now replaced the heavy yurts of the

steppe, while Indian and European cloth replaced the *ikats* and appliqués of Central Asia. Gulbadan Begum (*c.*1523–1603), daughter of Babur, wrote that the tent lining was of Gujarati cloth of gold, whereas the 'covering of the pavilions and of the large audience tent was, inside, European brocade, and outside Portuguese cloth. The tent poles were gilded; that was very ornamental.'

The Mughal Empire was to last for more than 300 years until its overthrow in 1858. It fought to keep Kabul at all costs, building a road through the Khyber Pass and more successfully relying on money rather than arms to keep control of the passes. However, the region north of the Hindu Kush remained under Uzbek control and the Safavids took Herat, while the southern region saw the rise of different Pashtun tribes (in Pakistan and India), a pattern of control that was to prove crucial in the making of modern Afghanistan.

The white marble mosque dedicated by Shah Jahan (1592–1666) during his visit to Babur's grave in Kabul in 1647. An original marble inscription refers to 'this theatre of heaven, the light garden of the angel king.' Photo: Bill Woodburn.

Chapter 8

The Creation of Modern Afghanistan

Coloured drawing of Ahmad
Shah Durrani (1722–72),
widely considered to be
the founder of modern
Afghanistan. Detail from an
Islamic album leaf, Deccan
school, 18th century. British
Museum, 1974,0617,0.17.25.

The creation of modern Afghanistan begins in the eighteenth century, and illustrates the rise in importance of the southern tribes. The two main Pashtun groups were the rival Ghilzai and Abdali (later Durrani). In 1709 Mir Wais Hotak (1673–1715), the Ghilzai governor of Kandahar, revolted against his Safavid rulers and defeated the Persian armies sent against him. After his death his son Mahmud seized power from his uncle and invaded Iran. The city of Isfahan was ravaged and the nobility slaughtered; however, Mahmud grew ever eccentric and was eventually murdered by his own troops.

In 1736 the increasingly powerful Turkmen commander of the Safavid armies, Nadir Quli Beg (1688–1747), took the throne of Persia and titled himself Nadir Shah. He backed the Abdali tribe and Ahmad Khan (1722–72), the teenage son of a leading Abdali chieftain, soon became commander of his bodyguard and guardian of his treasury. Nadir took Kandahar after a year-long siege and destroyed it in 1738, founding a nearby replacement city in his name. The strategic Ghilzai fortress known as Kalat-i Ghilzai was levelled (although it was later rebuilt by the British). He then marched on the Mughals, capturing Kabul and sacking Delhi (where he looted the Koh-i Noor Diamond – a famous diamond now in the British Crown jewels – and the Mughal emperor's golden Peacock Throne) in 1739, and leaving a bitter memory as his name entered the Indian language as synonymous with 'massacre'. Nadir Shah's Persian officers eventually assassinated him in June 1747, but Ahmad Khan retained his treasury and was backed by an experienced Afghan fighting force. A *jirga* (council) elected him their ruler with the title of Ahmad Shah, Dur-i Durran ('Pearl of Pearls'), and crowned him with a wheat-sheaf garland, an act which is commemorated by the inclusion of two wheat sheaves on the modern Afghan flag.

Ahmad Shah Durrani re-founded Kandahar as his own capital, with a grid of streets inside massive defences that lasted as late as the 1940s: it was called Ahmadshahi, but nicknamed *ashraf u'l-bilad* ('foremost of cities'). He took Balkh and Badakhshan and extended his kingdom from Khurasan to Kashmir, and from the Amu Darya to the Arabian Sea. He was the first real Afghan ruler, founding a dynasty that reigned until 1818, with the Durranis remaining powerful government players until 1973. He is therefore often credited with founding the nation-state of Afghanistan and is still known as Ahmad Shah Baba ('Father of Afghanistan'). Soon after his death in 1772, his second son Timur Shah (r. 1772–93) moved the capital to Kabul where it has remained ever since. He lost the support of the Pashtuns, however, and many of his father's achievements disappeared through tribal struggles.

The following period coincides with increasing British interest in the riches of India. The defeat of Napoleon left Russia as a potential rival, but Afghanistan was viewed as a useful buffer region between the two powers. The British East India Company administrator Mountstuart Elphinstone (1779–1859) was sent there in 1809 at the head of a delegation and commented:

> *The internal government of the tribes answers its end so well that the utmost disorders of the royal government never derange its operations, nor disturb the lives of the people. A number of organized and high-spirited republics are ready to defend their rugged country against a tyrant; and are able to defy the feeble efforts of a party in a civil war.*

This was consistent with what he was told by one Afghan: 'We are content with discord, we are content with alarms, we are content with blood, we will never be content with a master.'

By 1826 Dost Mohammad Khan (1793–1863) had seized power in Kabul. He was popular locally but his negotiations with Russia and his desire to regain the Punjab, now part of the expanding British-supported Sikh kingdom founded by Maharaja Ranjit Singh, the 'Lion of Lahore' (1780–1839), led to the Governor-General of India, Lord Auckland (1784–1849), deciding to replace him by someone more malleable. The terms of a new treaty stated:

> *When the Shah shall have established his authority in Kabool and Kandahar, he will annually send the Maharaja the following articles: viz. 55 high-bred horses, of approved colour and pleasant paces, 11 Persian scimitars* [a type of sword], *7 Persian poniards* [a dagger typically having a slender square or triangular blade], *25 good mules, fruits of various kinds, both dry and fresh, and sirdas or musk melons, of a sweet and delicate flavour (to be sent throughout the year), by the way of the Kabool River to Peshawar; grapes, pomegranates, apples, quinces, almonds, pistahs, or chionuts* [pistachios], *an abundant supply of each; as well as pieces of satin of every colour; chogas* [overcoats] *of fur, kim khabs* [textiles] *wrought with gold and silver, and Persian carpets, altogether to the number of 101 pieces.*

The First Anglo-Afghan War (1839–1842) had begun. The 'Army of the Indus', made up of over 15,000 British and Indian troops, 38,000 camp-followers (including bearers, cooks, laundry-men and farriers) and a huge camel-train to take the ammunition and personal supplies, soon took Kandahar, where the former Durrani ruler Shah Shuja (c.1785–1842) was restored as amir on 8 May 1839. However, a British captain witnessing the event concluded: 'Unless I have been deceived, all the national enthusiasm of the scene was entirely confined to His Majesty's immediate retainers.

The people of Kandahar viewed the whole affair with the most mortifying indifference.' Expecting equally easy progress, the British left their heavy cannon behind and marched on Ghazni. They were shocked at the scale of the defences and the fact that the standard-issue Brown Bess musket was out-ranged by skilful local use of long-barrelled matchlock rifles (*jezail*). Nevertheless, Ghazni was successfully stormed, and Kabul fell soon afterwards and almost without a shot.

Peace was short-lived. The Kandahar garrison began to encounter tough resistance, and in November 1841 Dost Mohammad's son, Wazir Akbar Khan (1813–45), led a revolt in Kabul. A mob overwhelmed the residence of the British envoy, Sir Alexander Burnes (1805–41), and hacked him and his companions

The mausoleum of Ahmad Shah Durrani at Kandahar. 'The king of high rank, Ahmad Shah Durrani, was equal to Kisra in managing the affairs of his government' (Dupree, 1980). Coloured drawing by James Rattray, an officer in the British East India Company army, *c.*1848. 37 x 25.9 cm. British Library, X562(27); © The British Library Board.

The tomb of Timur Shah in Kabul. This 18th century Mughal-style monument was described in 1839 by the British traveller James Atkinson as 'still unfinished; it is a mere shell, built of burnt brick unplastered, and without minarets or embellishment of any kind . . . The walls and cupola bear innumerable marks of cannon-balls and shot.' It was badly destroyed in the civil war (1992–1994) but has since been restored by the Aga Khan Trust for Culture. Photo: Aga Khan Trust for Culture.

to death, leaving parts of his body hanging in his garden for months. Negotiations failed and snow prevented the arrival of a relief brigade from Kandahar. The remaining British delegation of 700 Europeans, 3,800 Indian troops and 12,000 camp followers finally retreated from the city on 6 January 1842 under constant fire and in freezing conditions. Only one Englishman, Dr Brydon, survived and the catastrophe shocked London, prompting the return the following year of a British 'Army of Retribution'. This destroyed the rebel base at Istalif north of Kabul and blew up the citadel at Ghazni, as well as the historical bazaar in Kabul, but quietly allowed Dost Mohammad to return to the citadel of the Bala Hissar ('High Fort'). His popularity enhanced, Dost Mohammad re-unified the country, taking Kandahar (1855), Balkh and the northern plains, and finally Herat after a ten-month siege (1863).

In 1869, following another civil war, Dost Mohammad's nominated successor and third son, Shir Ali (1825–79), came to the throne amid tension over the gradual Russian advance into Central Asia and their annexation of Bukhara and Samarkand. This was the height of the 'Great Game', the struggle between Britain and Russia for domination of Central Asia as immortalized by Rudyard Kipling in his novel *Kim* (1901) and summed up in Tate's *The Kingdom of Afghanistan: A Historical Sketch* (1911) as follows: 'Between the Russian Dominions in Asia and the Indian Empire of Great Britain, Afghanistan is placed, like a nut, between the levers of a cracker.'

The arrival of a Russian mission in Kabul in 1878 triggered the Second Anglo-Afghan War (1878–1880), as the British sent troops into the country and insisted on a permanent residency in the city.

On 3 September 1879 rioting Afghan soldiers murdered the new British envoy, Sir Louis Cavagnari (1841–79), along with most of his escort in the Bala Hissar. This led to an army commanded by General Sir Frederick Roberts (1832–1914) rapidly occupying Kabul. A rebellion flared up in protest, and a British brigade was routed at Maiwand near Kandahar in July 1880 by an Afghan force commanded by Ayub Khan (1857–1914), a son of Shir Ali. Roberts responded quickly, relieved the British garrison in Kandahar, and defeated the Afghan army the next day while Ayub Khan watched in dismay from Babur's nearby monument at Chihl Zina (p. 127).

In the same year, Abdur Rahman Khan (1840–1901) – a grandson of Dost Mohammad – was proclaimed Amir of Kabul by a tribal council and endorsed by the British on condition that he supported them. This marks the next stage in the creation of modern Afghanistan as Abdur Rahman ('Iron Amir') subdued, exiled and resettled tribes within borders drawn up by Russia and Britain. In 1895 he also succeeded where many others, including the Emperor Timur (see p. 124), had failed and subdued the fiercely independent pagan tribes of the eastern region of Kafiristan ('Land

View of the fortified town and citadel of Ghazni by James Rattray, c. 1848. This view is looking from the west side and was drawn shortly before the fortifications were destroyed during the First Anglo-Afghan War. Coloured lithograph print, 39 x 29.7 cm. British Library, X562(18); © The British Library Board.

of the Infidel'). These were forcibly converted to Islam and the region accordingly renamed Nuristan ('Land of Light').

Despite his success in forging a unified country, Abdur Rahman foresaw larger political problems ahead when he wrote: 'How can a small power like Afghanistan, which is like a goat between two lions, or a grain of wheat between two strong millstones of the grinding mill, stand in the midway of the stones without being ground to dust?' In February 1884 British political and military fears of Russian designs on India began to simmer again when Turkmen tribal elders in the Merv Oasis surrendered to a Russian military delegation headed by Lieutenant Alikhanov. Matters came to a head the next year when Russian troops advanced along the Murghab river and drove off an Afghan force commanded by General Ghaws ud-Din Khan near Penjdeh, on Afghanistan's north-west frontier. The Russians signed a treaty in 1887 whereby Penjdeh was declared part of Russian territory and the former border reconfirmed (and continuing until today). The south-west border with Iran had already been acknowledged in 1872, and in 1893 the border with India (later Pakistan) was defined by the so-called Durand Line, which cut through traditional Pashtun tribal territories and continues to be contested.

Then, as now, it was the local tribes who particularly felt the effects of these political decisions. In the north, the loss of pasture because of lines drawn on a map obliged many Turkmen nomads within Afghanistan to adopt a semi-nomadic or fully settled existence, a heart-wrenching blow because, in the words of a much earlier medieval writer, 'the steppe is father and mother to them, just as towns are to us'. The other main tribes in the northern region were Uzbeks and Tajiks. Like the Turkmen, the Uzbeks have a complicated early history, but they probably entered from Turkic Central Asia in the wake of the Mongol invasion and were strengthened by successive waves from the fourteenth century onwards. Although some continued to maintain a nomadic existence until recently, most had already settled by the nineteenth century and thrived as merchants and craftsmen in the towns. The Tajiks, on the other hand, are Iranian-speakers and they probably represent an older population substrate; they are rather confusingly often referred to in nineteenth century literature as 'Sarts' along with Kirghiz and Kazakh nomads. There were also significant numbers of Jewish craftsmen in the towns. Other ethnic groups included the Hazaras in the central Hindu Kush (who speak Persian but are of Turko-Mongolian origin) and Aimaks in the west and north-west, whereas in the southern regions the main tribes are Pashtun (who speak Pashto, an Iranian language) with smaller numbers of Baluch.

Within Afghanistan the earliest photographs and surviving ethnographic items, ranging from clothing and personal adornment to horse trappings and tent fittings, date from the late nineteenth century. These confirm a strong sense of tribal and regional identity. Variations extend from preferred colours to embroidery styles, motifs and the type of appliqué.

Below Painted portrait of Dost Muhammad Khan (1793–1863), the powerful Afghan ruler who was regarded as a sufficient threat by the British to trigger the First Anglo-Afghan War in 1839. Gouache on cardboard, Anon., c.1850. Diam. 3.3 cm. British Museum, 1982,0622,0.2.4, donated by Mrs E. Hollinrake.

Uzbek yurt hanging with Russian printed cotton lining. Northern Afghanistan, 64 x 11 cm. British Museum, 1997,02.3.

Rams' horns, for instance, are common in the northern regions and reflect a steppe tradition that may extend far back in time. Floral motifs, peacocks (representing wealth) and water ewers (symbolizing life and ritual purity) feature on Uzbek embroidery, whereas tulips (the first steppe plant to flower after rain) are a typical Turkmen motif. Mirrors and coins are popular amuletic or protective attachments on Pashtun and Baluch embroidery, while a wider selection of talismans ranging from buttons or keys to tufts of hair, snake designs or triangle motifs are typical of Turkmen children's shifts (*kurta*). Particular colours were considered to protect from evil or danger, notably blue, which is believed to ward off the evil eye and perhaps explaining the propensity for turquoise on personal ornaments found in the first-century nomad graves at Tillya Tepe (see p. 71). The beads on many ethnographic items were imported from Czechoslovakia (later superseded by India), and the range of coins gives an interesting insight into circulation patterns typically containing a mix of Afghan, Russian, Persian and Indian currency. However, very few items of this period are signed or dated and attributing place of production is difficult. Moreover, defining ethnicity is complex. Many categories of material culture cross ethnic groups, and it is unlikely that all of the jewellery that can be classified as, for example, Turkmen was only made by Turkmen. Moreover, tribal styles cross modern borders and there is little to differentiate between the work of Turkmen or Uzbeks in Afghanistan and their modern neighbours to the north.

Typical items sold in urban bazaars included mulberry-wood bowls, glazed lamps, copper water-pipes, teapots and water jugs (with engraved decoration and dragon-headed handles derived from Timurid forerunners), and ceramic plates decorated with slip painting and splash-glazed *sgraffiato* (again successors of earlier medieval traditions). Some pottery was inscribed with pious mottos illustrating the types of food being consumed. For example: 'From the beginning, when He [Allah] made paradise, He determined fates. May he who eats *palov* [a rice and meat dish] from this plate eat his fill. Likewise may he who eats *shorba* [soup] from this plate eat his fill.' However, many Afghans lived in the countryside and never went to these bazaars. In these cases, the dual role of itinerant craftsmen and domestic production was crucial because few villages could support full-time craftsmen other than blacksmiths. This led to the creation of a small number of settled communities of specialists who marketed their goods and skills according to the different seasons: they include potters, knife-smiths, leatherworkers, carpenters, weavers, threshers, sieve-makers and pedlars. One pedlar summed up his adaptability to the market: 'One day I am a *chaj* [winnowing tray]-maker, another day I am a cloth-seller, depending on my fortune. Even right now we cannot tell. Yesterday this man was one, today he is the second and tomorrow he may be the third.'

For these individuals and their rural customers, barter was a common form of transaction (as it probably had been for thousands of years), although cash was used to invest in large amounts of local products such as cumin, aloeswood, nuts and therapeutic mushrooms which were a lucrative trade item to British India. Writing in 1896, the British East India Company administrator Sir George Scott Robertson commented:

Brass container for eye make-up with an embroidered cloth cover. This is Baluch work from the Ghazni region, late 20th century. It was acquired in Afghanistan by M.G. Konieczny. 70 x 40 cm. British Museum, 1973,07.8.

Portrait photograph of King Amanullah (1892–1960) in traditional dress with a hunting rifle. He accelerated his father's attempts to modernize Afghanistan, travelled abroad and founded the country's national museum. 13.6 cm x 8.5 cm. British Museum, Lynch.2, donated by Mrs C. Lynch.

The pedlars are few in number. They bring all manner of trashy goods into the country – sham jewellery, imitation kinob, common kullahs [a local form of pointed hat], *cotton velvet, cheap silks, glass beads, brass thimbles, sometimes with English inscriptions on them, and all manner of worthless-looking small articles for personal adornment.*

From the late nineteenth century onwards, the Afghan, Iranian and Central Asian markets became dominated by Russian exports either coming across the Caspian or via the Transcaspian railway: the wares included porcelain (some with mottos inspired by their new customers), metal items, samovars, lacquered wooden bowls and cheap cloth printed with floral or *ikat* [resist-dyed] designs. Commenting on the effects of this, the author Fritz Machatschek wrote:

The importation of cheap Russian mass products resulted first in a quantitative, but soon after also in a qualitative, decrease of the local trade. It degenerated into a skill which was practised solely to make money easily and quickly. Artisans tried to copy inferior European products, introduced European patterns, colours and machines, and ended up by losing all connection with Art.

In the meantime, other effects of the European industrial revolution were beginning to be witnessed in Afghanistan. In 1901 Abdur Rahman Khan was succeeded by his eldest son Habibullah (1872–1919). He declared a general amnesty on everyone banished by his father and began to modernize the country; the reforms included the establishment of the first secular schools and a redevelopment of infrastructure, including the first telephone lines. State-run steam-powered workshops known as the *Mashin-khana*, located just south of the capital, manufactured goods ranging from heavy artillery to coins and woollen items. The national printing press here produced an influential nationalist Islamic periodical, *Seraj ul-akhbar-e afghaniya* ('*The Torch of Afghan News*'), edited by former exile to Turkey, Mahmud Tarzi (1865–1933). In addition to these and more frivolous innovations such as the introduction of golf, Habibullah rejected the Anglo-Russian Convention of 1907, which declared Afghanistan to be a buffer state between the empires of Great Britain and Russia, and tentatively sought relations with the Germans, Turks and Bolsheviks.

Photograph of Muhammad Nadir Shah (1883–1933) who ended a chaotic period of rule after the death of King Amanullah and ruled Afghanistan briefly from 1929 to 1933. He founded Kabul University in 1932 but was murdered by a student the following year. 13.2 cm x 8.6 cm. British Museum, Lynch.6, donated by Mrs C. Lynch.

In 1919 Habibullah was murdered on a hunting trip near Jalalabad, and after a brief struggle was succeeded by his third son Amanullah (1892–1960) who later adopted the title of king. He provoked the British into the Third Anglo-Afghan War in 1919, when the Royal Air Force introduced aerial bombing to the country, but after only three weeks of fighting a treaty was agreed granting Afghanistan full control over its diplomatic relations. This marks the moment at which many Afghans feel that they finally became independent of Britain. The Soviet Union was the first country to recognize the new state, and in return the Afghans were the first neighbouring country to recognize the Bolshevik government. Amanullah toured abroad for eight months. He was impressed by the sweeping reforms instituted by Kemal Atatürk (1881–1938) in Turkey and Reza Khan (1878–1944) in Iran, and he planned a new Westernized capital at Darulaman, south-west of the old city of Kabul. The scheme included palaces, government buildings, a theatre, cafes and trolleybuses. It was here too that a building designed for the Municipality was used as the site of a new national museum in 1931, replacing the former royal collection originally housed in Abdur Rahman's Moon Palace and Amanullah's Royal Palace. The mayor of Berlin was requested to send architects and engineers but the designs failed to please and inspiration was instead sought from André Godard, the architect with the newly arrived French archaeological mission, whose ideas evoked the eighteenth century chateaux. Emerging nation-states, then as now, need historical identity and archaeology is the perfect tool to supply this. It is therefore not surprising that a treaty was now signed giving French archaeologists a temporary monopoly on archaeological research in the country, similar to that which they had previously enjoyed in neighbouring Iran, and excavations began the following year. The principal focus of these was art-historical and on sites that could provide information on the

The tomb of Nadir Shah in the centre of Kabul as its restoration nears completion. Photo: author.

eastward diffusion of Hellenism, the origin of Gandharan art and its relation to Buddhist art, and the extent of Silk Road trade through Afghanistan. Investigations were begun at many important sites, including Balkh, Bagram and Buddhist sites such as Bamiyan, Hadda, Shotorak and Fonduqistan.

Amanullah's social reforms offended conservatives, however, and a revolt led by the Tajik Habibullah Ghazi, popularly known as Bacha Saqqao ('Son of a Water Carrier') (c.1890–1929), forced him to flee with his family to Italy in 1929. After nine chaotic months Bacha Saqao and his followers were publicly hanged, then shot, and General Muhammad Nadir Shah (1883–1933), a Durrani Pashtun, was installed as ruler. After his assassination a few years later he was succeeded by his son, Muhammad Zahir Shah (1914–2007), who reigned until 1973, although his father's brothers effectively ran the country. His cousin and brother-in-law, General Mohammed Daoud (1909–18) was prime minister and played off the Soviet Union and the United States against each other at the height of the Cold War: both countries duly invested, with the Soviets concentrating on infrastructure projects while the Americans focused on grain and services. The Afghan army was reorganized along Red Army lines. In the meantime Lashkar Gah, the modern capital of Helmand province, became known popularly as 'Little America', and the first archaeological expeditions arrived from the American Museum of Natural History and the University Museum of the University of Pennsylvania. More than a hundred cave sites were surveyed for Palaeolithic remains, with the surprising discovery that some of these had been re-occupied in late historical periods by nomadic pastoralists (see p. 83). The approach of these expeditions was much more multi-disciplinary than before, including geologists, naturalists and physical anthropologists as well as archaeologists, and the ensuing reports

were among the first to include scientific analyses.

During this period of stability further educational reforms were made in the country, the veil made voluntary and constitutional democracy introduced. It was also a period of wider foreign assistance and this is reflected in the greater variety of archaeological expeditions. In 1957 Italian archaeologists began work at Ghazni, where they excavated the magnificent medieval palace of Mas'ud III, and explored the remains of an important Buddhist monastery at Tepe Sardar ('Prince's Mound', so named after being used as a campsite by Amir Habibullah). In the meantime, Afghanistan's cultural heritage was put on tour for the first time and an exhibition of objects from museums in Kabul and Ghazni opened in New York in 1966, before moving to Los Angeles, Washington and finally London in December 1967, where it sealed a newly agreed Anglo-Afghan Cultural Convention. Five years later the British Academy established the Society for Afghan Studies, with a (short-lived) British Institute in Kabul founded the following year and excavations began at Old Kandahar.

In July 1973 Mohammed Daoud declared himself president while King Zahir was abroad, but he and his family were later murdered and a new revolutionary Marxist regime was installed under Mohammad Taraki (1917–79) in April 1978. The previous over-reliance on foreign aid had created an economic crisis when aid began to slow down, and employment prospects could not keep up with the growing aspirations of the educated urban classes. Moreover, opinions were polarizing between educated left-wing ideologists and an increasingly strong traditional conservative movement. Rural revolts broke out in protest at proposed socialist land reform and equal education policies. An army division mutinied in Herat but was crushed by force. Taraki was replaced by his deputy, Hafizullah Amin (1929–79), who subsequently had

Opposite A floral print woman's dress with velvet skirt and silk embroidered cotton sleeves. The bodice is heavily decorated with coins, beads and buttons. This is typical of nomadic herders and gypsies known as Kuchi. 1980s, L. 115 cm; w. 142 cm. British Museum, 2008,6039.1.

Russian export porcelain teapot, inscribed 'Afghanistan'. This was made in a famous factory founded by Francis Gardner on 24 February 1766 in the Moscow district. This produced porcelain decorated in European or Chinese styles and dominated the export markets of Central Asia, Afghanistan and Iran. Late 19th or early 20th century. H. 13.1 cm. British Museum, 2002,0103.47, given by Lewis Baxter through The Art Fund.

Taraki smothered to death, but Moscow distrusted Amin. The Soviet army began pouring over the border on Christmas Eve 1979, with an air assault into Kabul followed by a motorized pincer movement from two directions, meeting at Kandahar. On 27 December 1979 Soviet special forces killed Hafizullah Amin, and Babrak Kamal (1921–96) was installed as president.

The situation soon spiralled out of control. The Soviets held the cities but lost the country. Their casualty rates climbed to over 15,000 men while the Afghan resistance was actively supported by Pakistan, Saudi Arabia and the United States, each with their own ideological agendas. Soviet troops drawn from Central Asian republics were replaced because their own comrades accused them of being local sympathizers, yet they were the subject of particular animosity from resentful *mujahideen* ('soldiers of God'), whom the Soviet soldiers termed *dukhi* ('ghosts'). Although the war unified the Afghans, the country's economy was wrecked, an estimated 1.5 million Afghans died, and 6 million were driven into exile, mainly into Pakistan and Iran. In 1992 the Russian journalist Artyom Borovik wrote that 'We thought that we were civilizing a backward country . . . but we rarely stopped to think how Afghanistan would influence us.' Worse was to follow. The withdrawal of the Soviet army in February 1989 was followed by the collapse of the Soviet Union and, in Afghanistan, eight years of ethnic civil war between powerful rival warlords inheriting huge weapons dumps. It was during this time that many historical and archaeological sites were looted or vandalized, and Kabul suffered most heavily, including repeated looting of the National Museum between 1992 and 1994, and the gutting of the upper floors during a rocket attack on the adjacent Presidential Palace (then occupied by the army) in May 1993.

These decades were the period when so-called 'war rugs'

became an expression of political events: woven by Baluch men, these carry stylized representations of modern military hardware combined with naïve depictions of the landscape or a map of Afghanistan. They were sold in the bazaars of Peshawar and Islamabad in neighbouring Pakistan and celebrated success and independence over the Soviet army. They went on to capture the moment in 2001 when planes flew into the World Trade Centre in New York.

In September 1996 the Taliban took Kabul and established an increasingly radical government within their new Islamic Emirate of Afghanistan. Women were banned from work and girls were no longer educated. Embroidery became, through necessity, an increasing expression of identity, but in this case made by women for men. Music and kite flying were banned, and a ban on human imagery was gradually extended to cover film, televisions, magazines and paintings. Heroic efforts were made by staff at Afghanistan's film institute to save their stock by hiding it behind a false wall, and a curator in the national art gallery used watercolours to transform oil-painted images into landscapes. Only a fortnight before the Taliban entered Kabul, over 3,000 objects packed in 500 containers were moved from the National Museum into temporary storage in the deserted Kabul Hotel and then to the Ministry of Information and Culture when the hotel was turned into an official guesthouse. But not all efforts were successful. In March 2001, the preservation of cultural heritage and tolerance of other faiths reached a particularly low point when

Coloured drawing by James Rattray entitled 'Ladies of Caubul in their in- and out-of-door costume', c.1848. The seated lady is shown with a water-pipe and personal effects and the vibrant colours of her dress contrast with the modest burqa of outdoor wear. The niches in the stucco-decorated walls behind were used to show off fragile and valuable porcelain. 27.5 x 17.5 cm. British Library, X562(24); © The British Library Board.

An Afghan war rug. This belongs to a long tradition of pictorial rugs produced by Baluchi weavers who began to depict the war in Afghanistan soon after the Soviet invasion in 1979. This example shows the outline of Afghanistan below the river Oxus at the top, with selected military hardware below, including the ubiquitous AK47 machine-gun. Wool, L. 96 cm; w. 60 cm. British Museum, 2010,6013.25, donated by Graham Gower.

a Taliban commander destroyed the large Buddhas at Bamiyan (see pp. 74, 79–80) on the grounds that they were 'idols' and therefore un-Islamic. The justification: 'Some people believe in these statues and pray to them . . . If people say these are not our beliefs, but only part of the history of Afghanistan, then all we are breaking are stones' (Mullah Omar, spiritual leader of the Taliban movement). The act was recorded on video for public broadcast, and over 2,000 figural depictions in museum collections were vandalized. This phase ended quickly in late 2001, when Western military support was given to a revitalized Northern Alliance assault, termed 'Operation Enduring Freedom', on the Taliban leadership for hosting Osama Bin Laden and his movement Al-Qaeda ('The Base'). A new constitution was signed, Hamid Karzai elected as president in 2004 and the process of reconstruction began.

The citadel at Herat, drawn in April 1885 by Colonel Sir Thomas Hungerford Holdich (1843–1929), then serving as part of the Russo-Afghan Boundary Commission. Holdich records that he drew this from the roof of 'one of the best houses of the local nobility' and reproduced it as the frontispiece of his book *The Indian Borderland* (1901). Private Collection.

Conclusion

Afghanistan is regularly described as the 'crossroads of Asia'. Although a clichéd phrase, it is appropriate in that it highlights the country's position as a strategic gateway between Central Asia, the Middle East and South Asia. At different periods it has been pulled into the political, economic, cultural or religious orbit of one or the other of these key regions and commentators from each will have their own very different perspectives on Afghanistan. This is true not only of modern authors, including the present one, but also of more ancient written sources. Historians, like modern journalists, often concentrate on exceptional events and wars, and usually overlook everyday stories. However, when it includes the evidence of archaeology, material culture and the oral or eye-witness testimonies of contemporaries, history offers a powerful source of knowledge.

Nevertheless, the phrase 'crossroads of Asia' disguises the contribution of a resilient indigenous population to the country's long history and cultural development, and the extent to which incomers were either assimilated or rejected. This strength of Afghan spirit should not be underestimated and is captured in the following quotation from a ninth-century poem by Hanzala of Badghis:

> *If leadership rests inside the lion's jaw,*
> *So be it. Go, snatch it from his jaws.*
> *Your lot shall be greatness, prestige, honour and glory.*
> *If all fails, face death like a man.*

The scale of destruction in Afghanistan in the recent decades of conflict means that the process of reconstruction is going to be hard and slow. Nevertheless, there have been a number of positive developments indicating that all is not lost when it comes to preserving the history, archaeology and culture of the country.

Throughout the wars, valiant attempts were made by museum staff in Kabul to catalogue their holdings and keep secret the fact that items of precious metal, including all of the Tillya Tepe finds, had been hidden in a Treasury vault under the Presidential Palace as early as autumn 1989. In 1994 the now disbanded Society for the Preservation of Afghanistan's Cultural Heritage (SPACH) was founded in neighbouring Pakistan and, together with UNESCO, provided considerable assistance during a particularly difficult period.

However, 2003 was a turning point. This was the year that reconstruction of the National Museum of Afghanistan began and archaeological expeditions resumed. The Afghan government confirmed that many treasures from the National Museum of Afghanistan were safe, and a new inventory was created. A world tour of some of the museum's finest collections began in Paris in 2006, opening in London at the British Museum in March 2011. It not only created a positive profile for the country but also generated income for the museum and training opportunities for its staff. New displays include huge carved wooden statues from Nuristan (some of which had previously been chopped up as firewood during the civil war), Buddhist wall-paintings and objects returned from the black market.

Although the trade in stolen antiquities from Afghanistan is a major cause for concern, there have been several encouraging acts of restitution, including, most recently, the return of a large group of the Bagram ivories (p. 67) and a large statue of Buddha (pp. 90–91), all stolen from the National Museum during the civil war (1992–94).

Moreover, many countries and organizations have been working closely with Afghan counterparts to rebuild traditional skills in arts and crafts, restore old buildings and rehabilitate public spaces. These are vital steps forward in ensuring the future of Afghanistan's cultural heritage.

Timeline

*c.*3500 BC	Earliest lapis lazuli imported from Afghanistan to Iraq
2500 BC	Lapis lazuli used in the Royal Tombs at Ur
*c.*550–330 BC	Achaemenid Empire and date of the Oxus Treasure (now in the British Museum)
521–486 BC	Reign of Darius I; his Foundation Charter from Susa refers to lapis lazuli from Sogdiana
329 BC	Alexander crosses the Hindu Kush
*c.*250–125 BC	Greco-Bactrian kingdom founded by Diodotus I
167–145 BC	Eucratides I campaigns into northern India
145/144 BC	Ai Khanum sacked by Scythian nomads
*c.*138–127 BC	Greco-Bactrian rulers probably lose Merv to the Parthian king Phraates II
*c.*130 BC	Ai Khanum abandoned after second sack by the Yüeh-chih nomads
2ndC–1stC BC	Kushan kingdom founded
1stC	Date of the tombs at Tillya Tepe
1stC–early 2ndC	Date of the strongrooms at Bagram
*c.*113–127	Reign of the great Kushan king Vima Kadphises
*c.*127–150	Reign of Kushan ruler Kanishka I
224	Ardashir I founds the Sasanian Empire with his capital at Ctesiphon in central Iraq
262	Reference to the regions of Afghanistan on the Sasanian inscription of Shapur I at Naqsh-i Rustam in Iran
667	Arab armies take Herat and Sistan
962–1186	Ghaznavid dynasty
*c.*1148–1206	Ghurid dynasty
1221	Mongols reach Afghanistan
1271	Marco Polo begins his travels
1333	Ibn Battuta travels through Afghanistan and records his impressions
1369–1404	Timur establishes the Timurid Empire with his capital at Samarkand
1404–1447	Reign of Shah Rukh and Herat made the new Timurid capital
1469–1506	Reign of Husain Baiqara; restoration of Herat

1747	Ahmad Shah Durrani establishes his capital at Kandahar
1776	Capital moved to Kabul
1839–1842	First Anglo-Afghan War
1878–1880	Second Anglo-Afghan War
1880–1901	Abdur Rahman Khan establishes a united Afghanistan
1901–1919	Amir Habibullah introduces modern innovations
1919–1929	King Amanullah regains control of foreign policy
1919	Third Anglo-Afghan War; first national museum established in Kabul
1922	Signature of Afghan-French archaeological collaboration and first archaeology
1933–1973	Reign of King Mohammed Nadir
1937, 1939	French excavations of the strongrooms at Bagram
1946	Kabul University founded
1966	Discovery of the treasure at Fullol; Museum of Islamic Art opened at Ghazni
1965–1978	French excavations at Ai Khanum
1973	Creation of the Republic of Afghanistan with the election of Mohammed Daoud
1978	Soviet excavations at Tillya Tepe
Dec 1979	Soviet army enters Afghanistan
1981	Museum at Hadda destroyed
1988	Highlights of the National Museum of Afghanistan put into storage in Kabul
1992–1994	Civil war; a rocket strike destroys the National Museum
March 2001	Taliban destroy the giant Buddhas of Bamiyan
March 2002	Exhibition tour begins at the Musée Guimet in Paris
2002	The minaret at Jam becomes the first UNESCO World Heritage Site in Afghanistan
2003	National Museum restored and re-opened

Further Reading

Ball, W. with Gardin, J. C., *Archaeological Gazetteer of Afghanistan/Catalogue des sites archéologiques d'Afghanistan*, Paris 1982

Ball, W., *Monuments of Afghanistan*, London 2008

Bosworth, C.E., *The Medieval History of Iran, Afghanistan and Central Asia*, London 1973

Clammer, P., *Lonely Planet Afghanistan*, Victoria 2007

Cribb, J. & Herrmann, G., eds, *After Alexander: Central Asia before Islam*, London 2007

Dupree, L., *Afghanistan*, Princeton 1980

Errington, E. & Cribb, J., *The Crossroads of Asia: Transformation in Image and Symbol of the Art of Ancient Afghanistan and Pakistan*, Cambridge 1992

Errington, E. & Sarkhosh Curtis, V., eds, *From Persepolis to the Punjab: Exploring Ancient Iran, Afghanistan and Pakistan*, London 2007

Hiebert, F. & Cambon, P., eds, *Afghanistan: Crossroads of the Ancient World*, London 2011

Holt, F. L., *Alexander the Great and Bactria: The Formation of a Greek Frontier in Central Asia*, Leiden 1988

Hopkirk, P., *The Great Game: On Secret Service in High Asia*, London 1990

Johnson, C. & Leslie, J., *Afghanistan: The Mirage of Peace*, London 2004

Knobloch, E., *The Archaeology and Architecture of Afghanistan*, Stroud 2002

Mascelloni, E., *War Rugs: The Nightmare of Modernism*, Milan 2009

Meissner, U., *Afghanistan: Hope and Beauty in a War-torn Land*, Munich 2008

Oleson, A., *Afghan Craftsmen: The Cultures of Three Itinerant Communities*, London 1994

Omrani, B. & Leeming, M., *Afghanistan: A Traveller's Companion and Guide*, Hong Kong 2005

Paine, S., *Embroidery from Afghanistan*, London 2006

Rasanayagam, A., *Afghanistan: A Modern History*, London 2010

Robinson, F., *The Mughal Emperors and the Islamic Dynasties of India, Iran and Central Asia*, London 2007

Simpson, St J., *The Begram Hoard: Indian Ivories from Afghanistan*, London 2011

Tanner, S., *Afghanistan: A Military History from Alexander the Great to the War Against the Taliban*, Philadelphia 2009 (revised edition)

Tissot, F., *Catalogue of the National Museum of Afghanistan*, Paris 2006

Vogelsang, W., *The Afghans*, London 2008 (revised edition)

Index